Scripture Union England & Wales
207–209 Queensway, Bletchley, Milton Keynes, MK2 2EB
info@scriptureunion.org.uk
www.scriptureunion.org.uk

British Library Cataloguing-in-Publication Data: a catalogue record for this book is available from the British Library.

*40 Days* uses Scripture quotations taken from The Holy Bible, New International Version (Anglicised edition). Copyright © 1979, 1984, 2011 by Biblica. Used by permission of Hodder & Stoughton Publishers, a Hachette UK company. All rights reserved.

This content has been adapted from material that first appeared in *Closer to God for Newcomers* (SU, 2012) written by Jo Swinney.

The right of Jo Swinney to be identified as author of this work has been asserted by her in accordance with the Copyright, Designs and Patents Act 1988.

Printed and bound in India by Thomson Press India Ltd
Designed by Max Randall

Scripture Union is an international Christian charity working with churches in more than 130 countries.

Thank you for purchasing this book. Any profits from this book support SU in England and Wales to bring the good news of Jesus Christ to children, young people and families and to enable them to meet God through the Bible and prayer.

Find out more about our work and how you can get involved at:
www.scriptureunion.org.uk (England and Wales)
www.suscotland.org.uk (Scotland)
www.suni.co.uk (Northern Ireland)
www.scriptureunion.org (USA)

## Welcome...

40 days isn't very long. But, it is long enough to take a journey through Matthew's Gospel whilst taking some time out to reflect, think and pray.

Matthew's Gospel takes us through the events of Jesus' life, records his teachings, his interactions with others and his Father God, and gives us a window into his thoughts and emotions. It puts him in the context of history and shows how he related to ancient prophecies concerning God's intention to rescue his people. You will be reading words on a page, but these words are living, and through them you will do more than learn about Jesus; you will have the opportunity to meet him for yourself.

The Jesus we will be meeting over the next 40 days is a carpenter's son and a king; he is God, and yet he is the ultimate man. He is a fiery preacher and a gentle guide; he is adored and reviled; he died and is alive. This Jesus claims to be God. If he is not, as CS Lewis pointed out, he must be mad or bad. Or could it be that he is what he says he is? This is the most important question in the world.

Now it's over to you.

Jo Swinney

# How to use this book

This book contains 40 excerpts from Matthew's Gospel, with plenty of space to help you reflect on, engage with and apply what you have read. If you have a Bible, you might want to read the book of Matthew from beginning to end – there's a lot more than we could include here and it will give you a fuller picture of Jesus' life and teachings.

Before you start reading, **take time to be quiet** and ask God to speak to you. Ask the Holy Spirit to bring the words to life.

**Get into the Bible...** Read the passage. What's the main point? What is God showing me about himself or about my life? Use the suggestions or questions to prompt reflection.

We have deliberately given you the space to ask big questions and to grapple honestly with God in prayer. Grab a pen to jot down thoughts or to underline words or phrases that stand out to you. There is plenty of space to **respond** to what God has shown you through journaling or prayer suggestions. You'll also find a number of questions and comments to consider along the way.

As you start this book, you might want to pray that the Holy Spirit will bring Matthew's Gospel to life, and that through these words you will get to know Jesus in a fresh and life-changing way.

¹⁸ This is how the birth of Jesus the Messiah came about: his mother Mary was pledged to be married to Joseph, but before they came together, she was found to be pregnant through the Holy Spirit. ¹⁹ Because Joseph her husband was faithful to the law, and yet did not want to expose her to public disgrace, he had in mind to divorce her quietly.

²⁰ But after he had considered this, an angel of the Lord appeared to him in a dream and said, 'Joseph son of David, do not be afraid to take Mary home as your wife, because what is conceived in her is from the Holy Spirit. ²¹ She will give birth to a son, and you are to give him the name Jesus, because he will save his people from their sins.'

²² All this took place to fulfil what the Lord had said through the prophet: ²³ 'The virgin will conceive and give birth to a son, and they will call him Immanuel' (which means 'God with us').

²⁴ When Joseph woke up, he did what the angel of the Lord had commanded him and took Mary home as his wife. ²⁵ But he did not consummate their marriage until she gave birth to a son. And he gave him the name Jesus.

Matthew 1:18–25

# Day 1

In the Bible, names carry huge significance. 'Immanuel', meaning 'God with us', is a theme that Matthew pursues throughout his account of Jesus' life, concluding with his words, 'Surely I am with you always...' (Matthew 28:20).

How can we tell if 'God is with us' today?

In times when life is hard, what difference does knowing that God is with us make?

Which part of this passage particularly strikes you?

What does God want to say to you through this passage?

. . . . . . . . . . . . . . . . . . . . . . . . . . . . . . . . . . . . . . . . . . . . . . . . . . . . . . . . . . .

. . . . . . . . . . . . . . . . . . . . . . . . . . . . . . . . . . . . . . . . . . . . . . . . . . . . . . . . . . .

. . . . . . . . . . . . . . . . . . . . . . . . . . . . . . . . . . . . . . . . . . . . . . . . . . . . . . . . . . .

. . . . . . . . . . . . . . . . . . . . . . . . . . . . . . . . . . . . . . . . . . . . . . . . . . . . . . . . . . .

. . . . . . . . . . . . . . . . . . . . . . . . . . . . . . . . . . . . . . . . . . . . . . . . . . . . . . . . . . .

. . . . . . . . . . . . . . . . . . . . . . . . . . . . . . . . . . . . . . . . . . . . . . . . . . . . . . . . . . .

. . . . . . . . . . . . . . . . . . . . . . . . . . . . . . . . . . . . . . . . . . . . . . . . . . . . . . . . . . .

. . . . . . . . . . . . . . . . . . . . . . . . . . . . . . . . . . . . . . . . . . . . . . . . . . . . .

Joseph is reassured by an angel that his son is spirit-conceived (v 20). We are asked to accept the truth of this mysterious story too, even as it contradicts everything we know about human reproduction.

Do you accept this truth? Why, or why not?

What do you want to say to God?

. . . . . . . . . . . . . . . . . . . . . . . . . . . . . . . . . . . . . . . . . . . . . . . . . . . . . . . . . . . . . . . . . . . . . . .

. . . . . . . . . . . . . . . . . . . . . . . . . . . . . . . . . . . . . . . . . . . . . . . . . . . . . . . . . . . . . . . . . . . . . . .

. . . . . . . . . . . . . . . . . . . . . . . . . . . . . . . . . . . . . . . . . . . . . . . . . . . . . . . . . . . . . . . . . . . . . . .

. . . . . . . . . . . . . . . . . . . . . . . . . . . . . . . . . . . . . . . . . . . . . . . . . . . . . . . . . . . . . . . . . . . . . . .

. . . . . . . . . . . . . . . . . . . . . . . . . . . . . . . . . . . . . . . . . . . . . . . . . . . . . . . . . . . . . . . . . . . . . . .

. . . . . . . . . . . . . . . . . . . . . . . . . . . . . . . . . . . . . . . . . . . . . . . . . . . . . . . . . . . . . . . . . . . . . . .

. . . . . . . . . . . . . . . . . . . . . . . . . . . . . . . . . . . . . . . . . . . . . . . . . . . . . . . . . . . . . . . . . . .

Consider the idea of God becoming man; the Creator of the universe nestled in Mary's womb. Let it blow your mind.

# Day 2

After Jesus was born in Bethlehem in Judea, during the time of King Herod, Magi from the east came to Jerusalem ² and asked, 'Where is the one who has been born king of the Jews? We saw his star when it rose and have come to worship him.'

³ When King Herod heard this he was disturbed, and all Jerusalem with him. ⁴ When he had called together all the people's chief priests and teachers of the law, he asked them where the Messiah was to be born. ⁵ 'In Bethlehem in Judea,' they replied, 'for this is what the prophet has written:

⁶ '"But you, Bethlehem, in the land of Judah,
    are by no means least among the rulers of Judah;
for out of you will come a ruler
    who will shepherd my people Israel."'

⁷ Then Herod called the Magi secretly and found out from them the exact time the star had appeared. ⁸ He sent them to Bethlehem and said, 'Go and search carefully for the child. As soon as you find him, report to me, so that I too may go and worship him.'

⁹ After they had heard the king, they went on their way, and the star they had seen when it rose went ahead of them until it stopped over the place where the child was. ¹⁰ When they saw the star, they were overjoyed. ¹¹ On coming to the house, they saw the child with his mother Mary, and they bowed down and worshipped him. Then they opened their treasures and presented him with gifts of gold, frankincense and myrrh. ¹² And having been warned in a dream not to go back to Herod, they returned to their country by another route.

Matthew 2:1–12

This new king, news of whose birth threw the current king into such a fluster, was announced in the heavens and worshipped by Magi from the east (v 11). His arrival was a cosmic event – for the Jews, yes, but really for the whole world, for us.

How does knowing that God sent his Son to earth out of his love for you make you feel?

. . . . . . . . . . . . . . . . . . . . . . . . . . . . . . . . . . . . . . . . . . .

. . . . . . . . . . . . . . . . . . . . . . . . . . . . . . . . . . . . . . . . . . .

. . . . . . . . . . . . . . . . . . . . . . . . . . . . . . . . . . . . . . . . . . .

. . . . . . . . . . . . . . . . . . . . . . . . . . . . . . . . . . . . . . . . . . .

. . . . . . . . . . . . . . . . . . . . . . . . . . . . . . . . . . . . . . . . . . .

. . . . . . . . . . . . . . . . . . . . . . . . . . . . . . . . . . . . . . . . . . .

. . . . . . . . . . . . . . . . . . . . . . . . . . . . . . . . . . . . . . . . . . .

. . . . . . . . . . . . . . . . . . . . . . . . . . . . . . . . . . . . . . . . . . .

. . . . . . . . . . . . . . . . . . . . . . . . . . . . . . . . . . . . . . . . . . .

. . . . . . . . . . . . . . . . . . . . . . . . . . . . . . . . . . . . . . . . . . .

. . . . . . . . . . . . . . . . . . . . . . . . . . . . . . . . . . . . . . . . . . .

. . . . . . . . . . . . . . . . . . . . . . . . . . . . . . . . . . . . . . . . . . .

. . . . . . . . . . . . . . . . . . . . . . . . . . . . . . . . . . . . . . . . . . .

# Day 2

What signs have brought you to worship King Jesus?

Reflect on the journey that has brought you to this place.

. . . . . . . . . . . . . . . . . . . . . . . . . . . . . . . . . . . . . . . . . . . . . . . . . . . . . . . . . . . . . . . . . . . .

. . . . . . . . . . . . . . . . . . . . . . . . . . . . . . . . . . . . . . . . . . . . . . . . . . . . . . . . . . . . . . . . . . . .

. . . . . . . . . . . . . . . . . . . . . . . . . . . . . . . . . . . . . . . . . . . . . . . . . . . . . . . . . . . . . . . . . . . .

. . . . . . . . . . . . . . . . . . . . . . . . . . . . . . . . . . . . . . . . . . . . . . . . . . . . . . . . . . . . . . . . . . . .

. . . . . . . . . . . . . . . . . . . . . . . . . . . . . . . . . . . . . . . . . . . . . . . . . . . . . . . . . . . . . . . . . . . .

. . . . . . . . . . . . . . . . . . . . . . . . . . . . . . . . . . . . . . . . . . . . . . . . . . . . . . . . . . . . . . . . . . . .

. . . . . . . . . . . . . . . . . . . . . . . . . . . . . . . . . . . . . . . . . . . . . . . . . . . . . . . . . . . . . . . . . . . .

. . . . . . . . . . . . . . . . . . . . . . . . . . . . . . . . . . . . . . . . . . . . . . . . . . . . . . . . . . . . . .

The Magi brought gold, frankincense and myrrh. What will you bring to Jesus?

In those days John the Baptist came, preaching in the wilderness of Judea [2] and saying, 'Repent, for the kingdom of heaven has come near.'

———

[13] Then Jesus came from Galilee to the Jordan to be baptised by John. [14] But John tried to deter him, saying, 'I need to be baptised by you, and do you come to me?'

[15] Jesus replied, 'Let it be so now; it is proper for us to do this to fulfil all righteousness.' Then John consented.

[16] As soon as Jesus was baptised, he went up out of the water. At that moment heaven was opened, and he saw the Spirit of God descending like a dove and alighting on him. [17] And a voice from heaven said, 'This is my Son, whom I love; with him I am well pleased.'

Matthew 3:1,2,13–17

# Day 3

Jesus presents himself for baptism; a sign of penitence and repentance.

Do you see how upside down this is?

. . . . . . . . . . . . . . . . . . . . . . . . . . . . . . . . . . . . . . . . . . . . . . . . . . . . . . . . . . . . . . . . . . . . . . . . . .

. . . . . . . . . . . . . . . . . . . . . . . . . . . . . . . . . . . . . . . . . . . . . . . . . . . . . . . . . . . . . . . . . . . . . . . . . .

. . . . . . . . . . . . . . . . . . . . . . . . . . . . . . . . . . . . . . . . . . . . . . . . . . . . . . . . . . . . . . . . . . . . . . . . . .

. . . . . . . . . . . . . . . . . . . . . . . . . . . . . . . . . . . . . . . . . . . . . . . . . . . . . . . . . . . . . . . . . . . . . .

How do you think you would have felt if you had been standing on the banks of the River Jordan when Jesus was baptised?

Why do you think Jesus identifies himself with the people facing judgement and not the God who does the judging? What does this mean for you?

Look back over the passage.
What does God want to say to you today?

. . . . . . . . . . . . . . . . . . . . . . . . . . . . . . . . . . . . . . . . . . . . . . . . . . . . . . . . . . . . . . .

. . . . . . . . . . . . . . . . . . . . . . . . . . . . . . . . . . . . . . . . . . . . . . . . . . . . . . . . . . . . . . .

. . . . . . . . . . . . . . . . . . . . . . . . . . . . . . . . . . . . . . . . . . . . . . . . . . . . . . . . . . . . . . .

. . . . . . . . . . . . . . . . . . . . . . . . . . . . . . . . . . . . . . . . . . . . . . . . . . . . . . . . . . . . . . .

. . . . . . . . . . . . . . . . . . . . . . . . . . . . . . . . . . . . . . . . . . . . . . . . . . . . . . . . . . . . . . .

. . . . . . . . . . . . . . . . . . . . . . . . . . . . . . . . . . . . . . . . . . . . . . . . . . . . . . . . . . . . . . .

. . . . . . . . . . . . . . . . . . . . . . . . . . . . . . . . . . . . . . . . . . . . . . . . . . . . . . . . . . . . . . .

. . . . . . . . . . . . . . . . . . . . . . . . . . . . . . . . . . . . . . . . . . . . . . . . . . . . . . . . . . . . . . .

# Day 4

Then Jesus was led by the Spirit into the wilderness to be tempted by the devil. ² After fasting for forty days and forty nights, he was hungry. ³ The tempter came to him and said, 'If you are the Son of God, tell these stones to become bread.'

⁴ Jesus answered, 'It is written: "Man shall not live on bread alone, but on every word that comes from the mouth of God."[Deut 8:3]'

⁵ Then the devil took him to the holy city and set him on the highest point of the temple. ⁶ 'If you are the Son of God,' he said, 'throw yourself down. For it is written:

"'He will command his angels concerning you,
    and they will lift you up in their hands,
    so that you will not strike your foot against a stone."[Ps 91:11,12]'

⁷ Jesus answered him, 'It is also written: "Do not put the Lord your God to the test."[Deut 6:16]'

⁸ Again, the devil took him to a very high mountain and showed him all the kingdoms of the world and their splendour. ⁹ 'All this I will give you,' he said, 'if you will bow down and worship me.'

¹⁰ Jesus said to him, 'Away from me, Satan! For it is written: "Worship the Lord your God, and serve him only."[Deut 6:13]'

¹¹ Then the devil left him, and angels came and attended him.

Matthew 4:1–11

Being a Christian means doing battle with temptation. What do you find particularly hard to resist?

Hebrews 4:15 says Jesus knew all temptations known to man. What are the temptations he is faced with here (vs 3,6,8)? Why would they have been particularly difficult for him?

. . . . . . . . . . . . . . . . . . . . . . . . . . . . . . . . . . . . . . . . . . . . .

. . . . . . . . . . . . . . . . . . . . . . . . . . . . . . . . . . . . . . . . . . . . .

. . . . . . . . . . . . . . . . . . . . . . . . . . . . . . . . . . . . . . . . . . . . .

. . . . . . . . . . . . . . . . . . . . . . . . . . . . . . . . . . . . . . . . . . . . .

. . . . . . . . . . . . . . . . . . . . . . . . . . . . . . . . . . . . . . . . . . . . .

. . . . . . . . . . . . . . . . . . . . . . . . . . . . . . . . . . . . . . . . . . . . .

. . . . . . . . . . . . . . . . . . . . . . . . . . . . . . . . . . . . . . . . . . . . .

. . . . . . . . . . . . . . . . . . . . . . . . . . . . . . . . . . . . . . . . . . . . .

. . . . . . . . . . . . . . . . . . . . . . . . . . . . . . . . .

# Day 4

Unlike Adam, Jesus resisted the devil. His primary defence was Scripture, and the Word of God is what will help us foil the attempts of the evil one to bring us down. Commit the following to memory:

**'If anyone is in Christ, the new creation has come: the old has gone, the new is here! All this is from God, who reconciled us to himself through Christ...'**

*(2 Corinthians 5:17)*

# Day 5

¹⁸ As Jesus was walking beside the Sea of Galilee, he saw two brothers, Simon called Peter and his brother Andrew. They were casting a net into the lake, for they were fishermen. ¹⁹ 'Come, follow me,' Jesus said, 'and I will send you out to fish for people.' ²⁰ At once they left their nets and followed him.

²¹ Going on from there, he saw two other brothers, James son of Zebedee and his brother John. They were in a boat with their father Zebedee, preparing their nets. Jesus called them, ²² and immediately they left the boat and their father and followed him.

Matthew 4:18–22

# Day 5

In Jewish culture at the time, a Rabbi – a teacher – would mentor a group of 'disciples', drawn from the elite students of the Torah. Why do you think Jesus chose his inner circle from common fishermen? How do you think they felt to be picked by him?

How does it feel to know that Jesus is calling you to follow him too?

. . . . . . . . . . . . . . . . . . . . . . . . . . . . . . . . . . . . . . . . . . . . . . . . . .

. . . . . . . . . . . . . . . . . . . . . . . . . . . . . . . . . . . . . . . . . . . . . . . . . .

. . . . . . . . . . . . . . . . . . . . . . . . . . . . . . . . . . . . . . . . . . . . . . . . . .

. . . . . . . . . . . . . . . . . . . . . . . . . . . . . . . . . . . . . . . . . . . . . . . . . .

. . . . . . . . . . . . . . . . . . . . . . . . . . . . . . . . . . . . . . . . . . . . . . . . . .

. . . . . . . . . . . . . . . . . . . . . . . . . . . . . . . . . . . . . . . . . . . . . . . . . .

. . . . . . . . . . . . . . . . . . . . . . . . . . . . . . . . . . . . . . . . . . . . . . . . . .

. . . . . . . . . . . . . . . . . . . . . . . . . . . . . . . . . . . . . . . . . . . . . . . . . .

. . . . . . . . . . . . . . . . . . . . . . . . . . . . . . . . . . . . . . . . . . .

Imagine: you're at work – work that provides for you, that you know how to do, that your family have done before you. Jesus comes along and calls to you. He wants you to go with him, leaving everything you know right then and there. What do you do?

. . . . . . . . . . . . . . . . . . . . . . . . . . . . . . . . . . . . . . . . . . . . . . . . . . . . . . . . . . . .

. . . . . . . . . . . . . . . . . . . . . . . . . . . . . . . . . . . . . . . . . . . . . . . . . . . . . . . . . . . .

. . . . . . . . . . . . . . . . . . . . . . . . . . . . . . . . . . . . . . . . . . . . . . . . . . . . . . . . . . . .

. . . . . . . . . . . . . . . . . . . . . . . . . . . . . . . . . . . . . . . . . . . . . . . . . . . . . . . . . . . .

. . . . . . . . . . . . . . . . . . . . . . . . . . . . . . . . . . . . . . . . . . . . . . . . . . . . . . . . . . . .

. . . . . . . . . . . . . . . . . . . . . . . . . . . . . . . . . . . . . . . . . . . . . . . . . . . . . . . . . . . .

. . . . . . . . . . . . . . . . . . . . . . . . . . . . . . . . . . . . . . . . . . . . . . . . . . . . . . . . . . . .

. . . . . . . . . . . . . . . . . . . . . . . . . . . . . . . . . . . . . . . . . . . . . . . . . . .

Sometimes following Jesus is hard work. He never promised it would be easy. Why is he still worth following, even when it's tough?

# Day 6

Now when Jesus saw the crowds, he went up on a mountainside and sat down. His disciples came to him, [2] and he began to teach them.

He said:

[3] 'Blessed are the poor in spirit,
for theirs is the kingdom of heaven.
[4] Blessed are those who mourn,
for they will be comforted.
[5] Blessed are the meek,
for they will inherit the earth.
[6] Blessed are those who hunger and thirst for righteousness,
for they will be filled.
[7] Blessed are the merciful,
for they will be shown mercy.
[8] Blessed are the pure in heart,
for they will see God.
[9] Blessed are the peacemakers,
for they will be called children of God.
[10] Blessed are those who are persecuted because of righteousness,
for theirs is the kingdom of heaven.

[11] 'Blessed are you when people insult you, persecute you and falsely say all kinds of evil against you because of me. [12] Rejoice and be glad, because great is your reward in heaven, for in the same way they persecuted the prophets who were before you.

Matthew 5:1–12

# Day 6

Work through the following list, jotting down your thoughts about how Jesus considers these people to be blessed. Ask him to help you understand the way things work when he is in charge.

• the poor in spirit

• those who mourn

• the meek

• those who hunger and thirst for righteousness

# Day 6

• the merciful                                   • the pure in heart

• the peacemakers                           • those who are persecuted

Look out for how God wants to bless you today.

⁷ And when you pray, do not keep on babbling like pagans, for they think they will be heard because of their many words. ⁸ Do not be like them, for your Father knows what you need before you ask him.

⁹ 'This, then, is how you should pray:

'"Our Father in heaven,
hallowed be your name,
¹⁰ your kingdom come,
your will be done,
    on earth as it is in heaven.
¹¹ Give us today our daily bread.
¹² And forgive us our debts,
    as we also have forgiven our debtors.
¹³ And lead us not into temptation,
    but deliver us from the evil one."

¹⁴ For if you forgive other people when they sin against you, your heavenly Father will also forgive you. ¹⁵ But if you do not forgive others their sins, your Father will not forgive your sins.

Matthew 6:7–15

# Day 7

Prayer needs to begin with a focus on who we are talking to, otherwise it quickly turns into a self-obsessed monologue. In prayer, we spend time in God's presence and discover more of who he is (vs 9,10).

What do you discover about who God is from the words of this prayer?

. . . . . . . . . . . . . . . . . . . . . . . . . . . . . . . . . . . . . . . . . . . . . .

. . . . . . . . . . . . . . . . . . . . . . . . . . . . . . . . . . . . . . . . . . . . . .

. . . . . . . . . . . . . . . . . . . . . . . . . . . . . . . . . . . . . . . . . . . . . .

. . . . . . . . . . . . . . . . . . . . . . . . . . . . . . . . . . . . . . . . . . . . . .

. . . . . . . . . . . . . . . . . . . . . . . . . . . . . . . . . . . . . . . . . . . . . .

. . . . . . . . . . . . . . . . . . . . . . . . . . . . . . . . . . . . . . . . . . . . . .

. . . . . . . . . . . . . . . . . . . . . . . . . . . . . . . . . . . . . . . . . . . . . .

. . . . . . . . . . . . . . . . . . . . . . . . . . . . . . . . . . . . . . . . . . . . . .

. . . . . . . . . . . . . . . . . . . . . . . . . . . . . . . . . . . . . . . . . . . . . .

. . . . . . . . . . . . . . . . . . . . . . . . . . . . . . . . . . . . . . . . . . . . . .

. . . . . . . . . . . . . . . . . . . . . . . . . . . . . . . . . . . . . . . . . . . . . .

. . . . . . . . . . . . . . . . . . . . . . . . . . . . . . . . . . . . . . . . . . . . . .

. . . . . . . . . . . . . . . . . . . . . . . . . . . . . . . . . . . . . . . . . . . . . .

. . . . . . . . . . . . . . . . . . . . . . . . . . . . . . . . . . . . . . . . . . . . . .

. . . . . . . . . . . . . . . . . . . . . . . . . . . . . . . . . . . . . . . . . . . . . .

. . . . . . . . . . . . . . . . . . . . . . . . . .

Make this prayer your own now. No matter how many times you may, or may not, have said it before, pray it through slowly, chewing over the meaning of the words as you say them.

You might find it helpful to write out the words of the prayer as you pray.

How did God bless you yesterday?

# Day 8

'Do not judge, or you too will be judged. [2] For in the same way as you judge others, you will be judged, and with the measure you use, it will be measured to you.

[3] 'Why do you look at the speck of sawdust in your brother's eye and pay no attention to the plank in your own eye? [4] How can you say to your brother, "Let me take the speck out of your eye," when all the time there is a plank in your own eye? [5] You hypocrite, first take the plank out of your own eye, and then you will see clearly to remove the speck from your brother's eye.

[6] 'Do not give dogs what is sacred; do not throw your pearls to pigs. If you do, they may trample them under their feet, and turn and tear you to pieces.

[7] 'Ask and it will be given to you; seek and you will find; knock and the door will be opened to you. [8] For everyone who asks receives; the one who seeks finds; and to the one who knocks, the door will be opened.

[9] 'Which of you, if your son asks for bread, will give him a stone? [10] Or if he asks for a fish, will give him a snake? [11] If you, then, though you are evil, know how to give good gifts to your children, how much more will your Father in heaven give good gifts to those who ask him! [12] So in everything, do to others what you would have them do to you, for this sums up the Law and the Prophets.

Matthew 7:1–14

# Day 8

What does Jesus want to convey about judging others?

How easy is it to avoid judging others in reality?

# Day 8

Remembering that God is your loving Father, ask him now for what you need (v 11).

. . . . . . . . . . . . . . . . . . . . . . . . . . . . . . . . . . . . . . . . . . . . . . . . . . . . . . . . . . . . . . .

. . . . . . . . . . . . . . . . . . . . . . . . . . . . . . . . . . . . . . . . . . . . . . . . . . . . . . . . . . . . . . .

. . . . . . . . . . . . . . . . . . . . . . . . . . . . . . . . . . . . . . . . . . . . . . . . . . . . . . . . . . . . . . .

. . . . . . . . . . . . . . . . . . . . . . . . . . . . . . . . . . . . . . . . . . . . . . . . . . . . . . . . . . . . . . .

. . . . . . . . . . . . . . . . . . . . . . . . . . . . . . . . . . . . . . . . . . . . . . . . . . . . . . . . . . . . . . .

. . . . . . . . . . . . . . . . . . . . . . . . . . . . . . . . . . . . . . . . . . . . . . . . . . . . . . . . . . . . . . .

. . . . . . . . . . . . . . . . . . . . . . . . . . . . . . . . . . . . . . . . . . . . . . . . . . . . . . . . . . . . . . .

. . . . . . . . . . . . . . . . . . . . . . . . . . . . . . . . . . . . . . . . . . . . . . . . . . . . . . . . . . . . . . .

. . . . . . . . . . . . . . . . . . . . . . . . . . . . . . . . . . . . . . . . . . . . . . . . . . . . . . . . . . . . . . .

. . . . . . . . . . . . . . . . . . . . . . . . . . . . . . . . . . . . . . . . . . . . . . . . . . . . . . .

Will God always give you what you ask for?

24 'Therefore everyone who hears these words of mine and puts them into practice is like a wise man who built his house on the rock. 25 The rain came down, the streams rose, and the winds blew and beat against that house; yet it did not fall, because it had its foundation on the rock. 26 But everyone who hears these words of mine and does not put them into practice is like a foolish man who built his house on sand. 27 The rain came down, the streams rose, and the winds blew and beat against that house, and it fell with a great crash.'
28 When Jesus had finished saying these things, the crowds were amazed at his teaching, 29 because he taught as one who had authority, and not as their teachers of the law.

Matthew 7:24–29

# Day 9

How can you build your life on the kind of foundations Jesus is talking about?

What are the rain, streams and winds in your life?
What do you need from God to help you stand firm?

.............................................................................
.............................................................................
.............................................................................
.............................................................................
.............................................................................
.............................................................................
.............................................................................
.............................................................................
.............................................................................
.............................................................................
.............................................................................
.............................................................................
.............................................................................

# Day 9

What words of Jesus have changed your life?

Are there any that you have held at a distance?
Ask him to help you with those teachings you struggle with.

# Day 10

⁵ When Jesus had entered Capernaum, a centurion came to him, asking for help. ⁶ 'Lord,' he said, 'my servant lies at home paralysed, suffering terribly.'

⁷ Jesus said to him, 'Shall I come and heal him?'

⁸ The centurion replied, 'Lord, I do not deserve to have you come under my roof. But just say the word, and my servant will be healed. ⁹ For I myself am a man under authority, with soldiers under me. I tell this one, "Go," and he goes; and that one, "Come," and he comes. I say to my servant, "Do this," and he does it.'

¹⁰ When Jesus heard this, he was amazed and said to those following him, 'Truly I tell you, I have not found anyone in Israel with such great faith. ...

———

¹³ Then Jesus said to the centurion, 'Go! Let it be done just as you believed it would.' And his servant was healed at that moment. ...

———

¹⁶ When evening came, many who were demon-possessed were brought to him, and he drove out the spirits with a word and healed all who were ill. ¹⁷ This was to fulfil what was spoken through the prophet Isaiah:

'He took up our infirmities
    and bore our diseases.'[Is 53:4]

Matthew 8:1–10,13,16,17

Israel has been waiting for a Messiah: someone to save them. Jesus is a powerful and convincing teacher, but could he be more than that?

. . . . . . . . . . . . . . . . . . . . . . . . . . . . . . . . . . . . . . . . . . . . . . . . . . . . . . . . . . . . . . . . . . . . . . . . . . . . . . . . . . . . . . . . . . .

. . . . . . . . . . . . . . . . . . . . . . . . . . . . . . . . . . . . . . . . . . . . . . . . . . . . . . . . . . . . . . . . . . . . . . . . . . . . . . . . . . . . . . . . . . .

. . . . . . . . . . . . . . . . . . . . . . . . . . . . . . . . . . . . . . . . . . . . . . . . . . . . . . . . . . . . . . . . . . . . . . . . . . . . . . . . . . . . . . . . . . .

. . . . . . . . . . . . . . . . . . . . . . . . . . . . . . . . . . . . . . . . . . . . . . . . . . . . . . . . . . . . . . . . . . . . . . . . . . . . . . . . . . . . . . . . . . .

. . . . . . . . . . . . . . . . . . . . . . . . . . . . . . . . . . . . . . . . . . . . . . . . . . . . . . . . . . . . . . . . . . . . . . . . . . . . . . . . . . . . . . . . . . .

. . . . . . . . . . . . . . . . . . . . . . . . . . . . . . . . . . . . . . . . . . . . . . . . . . . . . . . . . . . . . . . . . . . . . . . . . . . . . . . . . . . . . . . . . . .

. . . . . . . . . . . . . . . . . . . . . . . . . . . . . . . . . . . . . . . . . . . . . . . . . . . . . . . . . . . . . . . . . . . . . . . . . . . . . . .

Do you believe that Jesus can heal today?

# Day 10

Spend some time talking to Jesus about those you know who need his healing. Be bold in asking him to make them well. Be honest about how you feel and what you think.

......................................................

......................................................

......................................................

......................................................

......................................................

......................................................

......................................................

......................................................

......................................................

......................................................

......................................................

......................................................

Which part of this passage does God want you to notice today?

[23] Then he got into the boat and his disciples followed him.
[24] Suddenly a furious storm came up on the lake, so that the
waves swept over the boat. But Jesus was sleeping. [25] The
disciples went and woke him, saying, 'Lord, save us! We're going
to drown!'

[26] He replied, 'You of little faith, why are you so afraid?' Then
he got up and rebuked the winds and the waves, and it was
completely calm.

[27] The men were amazed and asked, 'What kind of man is this?
Even the winds and the waves obey him!'

Matthew 8:23–27

# Day 11

The disciples were spending all day every day with Jesus, and moment by moment he was expanding their concept of who he was.

How would you answer their question: 'What kind of man is this?'

. . . . . . . . . . . . . . . . . . . . . . . . . . . . . . . . . . . . . . . . . . . . . . . . . . . . . . . . . . . . . . . . . . . . . . . . . . . . . . . . . . . .

. . . . . . . . . . . . . . . . . . . . . . . . . . . . . . . . . . . . . . . . . . . . . . . . . . . . . . . . . . . . . . . . . . . . . . . . . . . . . . . . . . . .

. . . . . . . . . . . . . . . . . . . . . . . . . . . . . . . . . . . . . . . . . . . . . . . . . . . . . . . . . . . . . . . . . . . . . . . . . . . . . . . . . . . .

. . . . . . . . . . . . . . . . . . . . . . . . . . . . . . . . . . . . . . . . . . . . . . . . . . . . . . . . . . . . . . . . . . . . . . . . . . . . . . . . . . . .

. . . . . . . . . . . . . . . . . . . . . . . . . . . . . . . . . . . . . . . . . . . . . . . . . . . . . . . . . . . . . . . . . . . . . . . . . . . . . . . . . . . .

. . . . . . . . . . . . . . . . . . . . . . . . . . . . . . . . . . . . . . . . . . . . . . . . . . . . . . . . . . . . . . . . . . . . . . . . . . . . . . . . . . . .

. . . . . . . . . . . . . . . . . . . . . . . . . . . . . . . . . . . . . . . . . . . . . . . . . . . . . . . . . . . . . . . . . . . . . . . . . . . . . . . . . . . .

. . . . . . . . . . . . . . . . . . . . . . . . . . . . . . . . . . . . . . . . . . . . . . . . . . . . . . . . . . . . . . . . . . . . . . . . . . . . . . . . . . . .

. . . . . . . . . . . . . . . . . . . . . . . . . . . . . . . . . . . . . . . . . . . . . . . . . . . . . . . . . . . . . . . . . . . . . . . . . .

# Day 11

Write your thoughts about what you have learned so far through
Matthew about who Jesus is.

. . . . . . . . . . . . . . . . . . . . . . . . . . . . . . . . . . . . . . . . . . . . . . . . . . . . . . . . . . . .

. . . . . . . . . . . . . . . . . . . . . . . . . . . . . . . . . . . . . . . . . . . . . . . . . . . . . . . . . . . .

. . . . . . . . . . . . . . . . . . . . . . . . . . . . . . . . . . . . . . . . . . . . . . . . . . . . . . . . . . . .

. . . . . . . . . . . . . . . . . . . . . . . . . . . . . . . . . . . . . . . . . . . . . . . . . . . . . . . . . . . .

. . . . . . . . . . . . . . . . . . . . . . . . . . . . . . . . . . . . . . . . . . . . . . . . . . . . . . . . . . . .

. . . . . . . . . . . . . . . . . . . . . . . . . . . . . . . . . . . . . . . . . . . . . . . . . . . . . . . . . . . .

. . . . . . . . . . . . . . . . . . . . . . . . . . . . . . . . . . . . . . . . . . . . . . . . . . . . . . . . . . . .

. . . . . . . . . . . . . . . . . . . . . . . . . . . . . . . . . . . . . . . . . . . . . . . . . . . . .

Flick back through the previous pages and notice how
God has spoken to you.

# Day 12

Jesus stepped into a boat, crossed over and came to his own town. ² Some men brought to him a paralysed man, lying on a mat. When Jesus saw their faith, he said to the man, 'Take heart, son; your sins are forgiven.'

³ At this, some of the teachers of the law said to themselves, 'This fellow is blaspheming!'
⁴ Knowing their thoughts, Jesus said, 'Why do you entertain evil thoughts in your hearts? ⁵ Which is easier: to say, "Your sins are forgiven," or to say, "Get up and walk"? ⁶ But I want you to know that the Son of Man has authority on earth to forgive sins.' So he said to the paralysed man, 'Get up, take your mat and go home.' ⁷ Then the man got up and went home. ⁸ When the crowd saw this, they were filled with awe; and they praised God, who had given such authority to man.

Matthew 9:1–8

When Jesus looked at the man he didn't only see his physical disability, he saw his sin (v 2). He knew what was going on in the hearts of the other people present too (v 4). Jesus sees everything about us, and chooses to forgive.

What do you want to say to Jesus?

. . . . . . . . . . . . . . . . . . . . . . . . . . . . . . . . . . . . . . . . . . . . . . . . . . . . . . . .

. . . . . . . . . . . . . . . . . . . . . . . . . . . . . . . . . . . . . . . . . . . . . . . . . . . . . . . .

. . . . . . . . . . . . . . . . . . . . . . . . . . . . . . . . . . . . . . . . . . . . . . . . . . . . . . . .

. . . . . . . . . . . . . . . . . . . . . . . . . . . . . . . . . . . . . . . . . . . . . . . . . . . . . . . .

. . . . . . . . . . . . . . . . . . . . . . . . . . . . . . . . . . . . . . . . . . . . . . . . . . . . . . . .

. . . . . . . . . . . . . . . . . . . . . . . . . . . . . . . . . . . . . . . . . . . . . . . . . . . . . . . .

. . . . . . . . . . . . . . . . . . . . . . . . . . . . . . . . . . . . . . . . . . . . . . . . . . . . . . . .

. . . . . . . . . . . . . . . . . . . . . . . . . . . . . . . . . . . . . . . . . . . . . . . . . . . . . . . .

. . . . . . . . . . . . . . . . . . . . . . . . . . . . . . . . . . . . . . . . . . . . . . . . . . . . . . . .

. . . . . . . . . . . . . . . . . . . . . . . . . . . . . . . . . . . . . . . . . . . . . . . . . . . . . . . .

. . . . . . . . . . . . . . . . . . . . . . . . . . . . . . . . . . . . . . . . . . . . . . . . . . . . . . . .

. . . . . . . . . . . . . . . . . . . . . . . . . . . . . . . . . . . . . . . . . . . . . . . . . . . . . . . .

. . . . . . . . . . . . . . . . . . . . . . . . . . . . . . . . . . . . . . . . . . . . . . . . . . . . . . . .

. . . . . . . . . . . . . . . . . . . . . . . . . . . . . . . . . . . .

# Day 12

What have Jesus' words accomplished in your life?

. . . . . . . . . . . . . . . . . . . . . . . . . . . . . . . . . . . . . . . . . . . . . . . . . . . . . .

. . . . . . . . . . . . . . . . . . . . . . . . . . . . . . . . . . . . . . . . . . . . . . . . . . . . . .

. . . . . . . . . . . . . . . . . . . . . . . . . . . . . . . . . . . . . . . . . . . . . . . . . . . . . .

. . . . . . . . . . . . . . . . . . . . . . . . . . . . . . . . . . . . . . . . . . . . . . . . . . . . . .

. . . . . . . . . . . . . . . . . . . . . . . . . . . . . . . . . . . . . . . . . . . . . . . . . . . . . .

. . . . . . . . . . . . . . . . . . . . . . . . . . . . . . . . . . . . . . . . . . . . . . . . . . . . . .

. . . . . . . . . . . . . . . . . . . . . . . . . . . . . . . . . . . . . . . . . . . . . . . . . . . . . .

. . . . . . . . . . . . . . . . . . . . . . . . . . . . . . . . . . . . . . . . . . . . . . . . . .

Spend some time confessing the ways you have turned away from God lately. Then hear him say,

### 'Take heart, your sins are forgiven.'

[18] While he was saying this, a synagogue leader came and knelt before him and said, 'My daughter has just died. But come and put your hand on her, and she will live.' [19] Jesus got up and went with him, and so did his disciples.

[20] Just then a woman who had been subject to bleeding for twelve years came up behind him and touched the edge of his cloak. [21] She said to herself, 'If I only touch his cloak, I will be healed.'

[22] Jesus turned and saw her. 'Take heart, daughter,' he said, 'your faith has healed you.' And the woman was healed at that moment.

[23] When Jesus entered the synagogue leader's house and saw the noisy crowd and the people playing pipes, [24] he said, 'Go away. The girl is not dead but asleep.' But they laughed at him. [25] After the crowd had been put outside, he went in and took the girl by the hand, and she got up. [26] News of this spread through all that region.

Matthew 9:18–26

# Day 13

Try to imagine yourself in the character of the woman Jesus heals. Her condition meant that she was considered unclean, and she would make anyone she touched unclean too. What do you imagine she was thinking as she pushed through the crowds to get to Jesus?

.................................................................................

.................................................................................

.................................................................................

.................................................................................

.................................................................................

.................................................................................

.................................................................................

Instead of becoming unclean through her touch, Jesus makes her clean. Take time to fully understand that Jesus has made you clean too.

Imagine you are in the crowds around Jesus. What can you hear, see, smell?

Picture yourself reaching out to touch Jesus. He turns and sees you. What is the expression on his face? What does he say to you?

Reflect on this from Isaiah 1:18:
'**Come now, let us settle the matter,' says the** Lord. **'Though your sins are like scarlet, they shall be as white as snow.'**

# Day 14

<sup>25</sup> At that time Jesus said, 'I praise you, Father, Lord of heaven and earth, because you have hidden these things from the wise and learned, and revealed them to little children. <sup>26</sup> Yes, Father, for this is what you were pleased to do.
<sup>27</sup> 'All things have been committed to me by my Father. No one knows the Son except the Father, and no one knows the Father except the Son and those to whom the Son chooses to reveal him.
<sup>28</sup> 'Come to me, all you who are weary and burdened, and I will give you rest. <sup>29</sup> Take my yoke upon you and learn from me, for I am gentle and humble in heart, and you will find rest for your souls. <sup>30</sup> For my yoke is easy and my burden is light.'

Matthew 11:25–30

At the heart of Christianity is the invitation to come to God, through his Son Jesus. All that is required of us is a child-like response of acceptance (v 26).

How might your relationship with God change if you were more child-like?

. . . . . . . . . . . . . . . . . . . . . . . . . . . . . . . . . . . . . . . . . . . . . . . . . . . . . . . . . . . . . . . . . . . . . .

. . . . . . . . . . . . . . . . . . . . . . . . . . . . . . . . . . . . . . . . . . . . . . . . . . . . . . . . . . . . . . . . . . . . . .

. . . . . . . . . . . . . . . . . . . . . . . . . . . . . . . . . . . . . . . . . . . . . . . . . . . . . . . . . . . . . . . . . . . . . .

. . . . . . . . . . . . . . . . . . . . . . . . . . . . . . . . . . . . . . . . . . . . . . . . . . . . . . . . . . . . . . . . . . . . . .

. . . . . . . . . . . . . . . . . . . . . . . . . . . . . . . . . . . . . . . . . . . . . . . . . . . . . . . . . . . . . . . . . . . . . .

. . . . . . . . . . . . . . . . . . . . . . . . . . . . . . . . . . . . . . . . . . . . . . . . . . . . . . . . . . . . . . . . . . . . . .

. . . . . . . . . . . . . . . . . . . . . . . . . . . . . . . . . . . . . . . . . . . . . . . . . . . . . . . . . . . . . . . . . . . . . .

. . . . . . . . . . . . . . . . . . . . . . . . . . . . . . . . . . . . . . . . . . . . . . . . . . . . . . . . . . . . . . . . . . . . . .

. . . . . . . . . . . . . . . . . . . . . . . . . . . . . . . . . . . . . . . . . . . . . . . . . . . . . . . . . . . . . . . . . . . . . .

. . . . . . . . . . . . . . . . . . . . . . . . . . . . . . . . . . . . . . . . . . . . . . . . . . . . . . . . . . . . . . . . . . . . . .

# Day 14

Use the space to write your RSVP. How are you going to answer this invitation to come close, to find rest, to learn from a gentle and kind teacher?

That same day Jesus went out of the house and sat by the lake. [2] Such large crowds gathered round him that he got into a boat and sat in it, while all the people stood on the shore. [3] Then he told them many things in parables, saying: 'A farmer went out to sow his seed. [4] As he was scattering the seed, some fell along the path, and the birds came and ate it up. [5] Some fell on rocky places, where it did not have much soil. It sprang up quickly, because the soil was shallow. [6] But when the sun came up, the plants were scorched, and they withered because they had no root. [7] Other seed fell among thorns, which grew up and choked the plants. [8] Still other seed fell on good soil, where it produced a crop – a hundred, sixty or thirty times what was sown. [9] Whoever has ears, let them hear.'

---

[18] 'Listen then to what the parable of the sower means: [19] when anyone hears the message about the kingdom and does not understand it, the evil one comes and snatches away what was sown in their heart. This is the seed sown along the path. [20] The seed falling on rocky ground refers to someone who hears the word and at once receives it with joy. [21] But since they have no root, they last only a short time. When trouble or persecution comes because of the word, they quickly fall away.

[22] The seed falling among the thorns refers to someone who hears the word, but the worries of this life and the deceitfulness of wealth choke the word, making it unfruitful. [23] But the seed falling on good soil refers to someone who hears the word and understands it. This is the one who produces a crop, yielding a hundred, sixty or thirty times what was sown.'

Matthew 13:1–9,18–23

# Day 15

Next to each seed, write the reasons that the seed doesn't grow and flourish. And then consider whether your spiritual health is endangered by that same thing. What can you do to ensure that the message of the kingdom bears fruit in your life?

The seed on the path

The seed on rocky places

The seed among thorns

'Jesus, I have heard your message, through your word and through the testimony of your followers. Help me understand it, so that I can be like the seed that yields an amazing crop.'

# Day 16

[44] 'The kingdom of heaven is like treasure hidden in a field. When a man found it, he hid it again, and then in his joy went and sold all he had and bought that field.

[45] 'Again, the kingdom of heaven is like a merchant looking for fine pearls. [46] When he found one of great value, he went away and sold everything he had and bought it.

Matthew 13:44–46

In what sense is the kingdom of heaven hidden (v 44)?
How did you come to find it?

. . . . . . . . . . . . . . . . . . . . . . . . . . . . . . . . . . . . . . . . . . . . . . . .

. . . . . . . . . . . . . . . . . . . . . . . . . . . . . . . . . . . . . . . . . . . . . . . .

. . . . . . . . . . . . . . . . . . . . . . . . . . . . . . . . . . . . . . . . . . . . . . . .

. . . . . . . . . . . . . . . . . . . . . . . . . . . . . . . . . . . . . . . . . . . . . . . .

. . . . . . . . . . . . . . . . . . . . . . . . . . . . . . . . . . . . . . . . . . . . . . . .

. . . . . . . . . . . . . . . . . . . . . . . . . . . . . . . . . . . . . . . . . . . . . . . .

. . . . . . . . . . . . . . . . . . . . . . . . . . . . . . . . . . . . . . . . . . . . . . . .


What value do you place on your relationship with Jesus?
Is there anything you value more?

. . . . . . . . . . . . . . . . . . . . . . . . . . . . . . . . . . . . . . . . . . . . . . . .

. . . . . . . . . . . . . . . . . . . . . . . . . . . . . . . . . . . . . . . . . . . . . . . .

. . . . . . . . . . . . . . . . . . . . . . . . . . . . . . . . . . . . . . . . . . . . . . . .

. . . . . . . . . . . . . . . . . . . . . . . . . . . . . . . . . . . . . . . . . . . . . . . .

. . . . . . . . . . . . . . . . . . . . . . . . . . . . . . . . . . . . . . . . . . . . . . . .

. . . . . . . . . . . . . . . . . . . . . . . . . . . . . . . . . . . . . . . . . . . . . . . .

. . . . . . . . . . . . . . . . . . . . . . . . . . . . . . . . . . . . . . . . . . . . . . . .


Ask God to reveal to you if there is anything you are holding on to at the expense of
living completely in his kingdom.

# Day 16

'*The world and its desires pass away, but whoever does the will of God lives for ever...*'

I John 2:17

[13] When Jesus heard what had happened, he withdrew by boat privately to a solitary place. Hearing of this, the crowds followed him on foot from the towns. [14] When Jesus landed and saw a large crowd, he had compassion on them and healed those who were ill.

[15] As evening approached, the disciples came to him and said, 'This is a remote place, and it's already getting late. Send the crowds away, so that they can go to the villages and buy themselves some food.'

[16] Jesus replied, 'They do not need to go away. You give them something to eat.'

[17] 'We have here only five loaves of bread and two fish,' they answered.

[18] 'Bring them here to me,' he said. [19] And he told the people to sit down on the grass. Taking the five loaves and the two fish and looking up to heaven, he gave thanks and broke the loaves. Then he gave them to the disciples, and the disciples gave them to the people.

[20] They all ate and were satisfied, and the disciples picked up twelve basketfuls of broken pieces that were left over. [21] The number of those who ate was about five thousand men, besides women and children.

Matthew 14:13–21

# Day 17

What does this passage add to the picture that Matthew is painting of Jesus?

. . . . . . . . . . . . . . . . . . . . . . . . . . . . . . . . . . . . . .

. . . . . . . . . . . . . . . . . . . . . . . . . . . . . . . . . . . . . .

. . . . . . . . . . . . . . . . . . . . . . . . . . . . . . . . . . . . . .

. . . . . . . . . . . . . . . . . . . . . . . . . . . . . . . . . . . . . .

. . . . . . . . . . . . . . . . . . . . . . . . . . . . . . . . . . . . . .

. . . . . . . . . . . . . . . . . . . . . . . . . . . . . . . . . . . . . .

. . . . . . . . . . . . . . . . . . . . . . . . . . . . . . . . . . . . . .

. . . . . . . . . . . . . . . . . . . . . . . . . . . . . . . . . . . . . .

. . . . . . . . . . . . . . . . . . . . . . . . . . . . . . . . . . . . . .

. . . . . . . . . . . . . . . . . . . . . . . . . . . . . . . . . . . . . .

. . . . . . . . . . . . . . . . . . . . . . . . . . . . . . . . . . . . . .

. . . . . . . . . . . . . . . . . . . . . . . . . . . . . . . . . . . . . .

. . . . . . . . . . . . . . . . . . . . . . . . . . . . . . . . . . . . . .

. . . . . . . . . . . . . . . . . . . . . . . . . . . . . . . . . . . . . .

. . . . . . . . . . . . . . . . . . . . . . . . . . . . . . . . . . . . . .

. . . . . . . . . . . . . . . . . . . . . . . . . . . . . . . . . . . . . .

. . . . . . . . . . . . . . . . . . . . . . . . . . . . . . . . . .

Jesus is compassionate. Even deep in his own sadness over the death of John the Baptist, he responds to the crowds with great love (v 14).

What do you have to offer – time, money, creativity, passion, a spare room or a talent for catering? Offer it to God, and watch with amazement what he can do with it.

Talk with God about what you have to offer, and ask him to take it and use it to his glory.

# Day 18

[22] Immediately Jesus made the disciples get into the boat and go on ahead of him to the other side, while he dismissed the crowd. [23] After he had dismissed them, he went up on a mountainside by himself to pray. Later that night, he was there alone, [24] and the boat was already a considerable distance from land, buffeted by the waves because the wind was against it.

[25] Shortly before dawn Jesus went out to them, walking on the lake. [26] When the disciples saw him walking on the lake, they were terrified. 'It's a ghost,' they said, and cried out in fear. [27] But Jesus immediately said to them: 'Take courage! It is I. Don't be afraid.'

[28] 'Lord, if it's you,' Peter replied, 'tell me to come to you on the water.'

[29] 'Come,' he said.

Then Peter got down out of the boat, walked on the water and came towards Jesus. [30] But when he saw the wind, he was afraid and, beginning to sink, cried out, 'Lord, save me!'

[31] Immediately Jesus reached out his hand and caught him. 'You of little faith,' he said, 'why did you doubt?'

[32] And when they climbed into the boat, the wind died down. [33] Then those who were in the boat worshipped him, saying, 'Truly you are the Son of God.'

Matthew 14:22–33

# Day 18

Peter was one of the first two disciples that Jesus called, and he came without hesitation, leaving everything behind (Matthew 4:18–20). Why do you think he asks Jesus to confirm who he is by calling him out onto the water (v 28)?

. . . . . . . . . . . . . . . . . . . . . . . . . . . . . . . . . . . . . . . . . . . . . . . . . . . . . . . . . . . . . . . . . . .

. . . . . . . . . . . . . . . . . . . . . . . . . . . . . . . . . . . . . . . . . . . . . . . . . . . . . . . . . . . . . . . . . . .

. . . . . . . . . . . . . . . . . . . . . . . . . . . . . . . . . . . . . . . . . . . . . . . . . . . . . . . . . . . . . . . . . . .

. . . . . . . . . . . . . . . . . . . . . . . . . . . . . . . . . . . . . . . . . . . . . . . . . . . . . . . . . . . . . . . . . . .

. . . . . . . . . . . . . . . . . . . . . . . . . . . . . . . . . . . . . . . . . . . . . . . . . . . . . . . . . . . . . . . . . . .

. . . . . . . . . . . . . . . . . . . . . . . . . . . . . . . . . . . . . . . . . . . . . . . . . . . . . . . . . . . . . . . . . . .

. . . . . . . . . . . . . . . . . . . . . . . . . . . . . . . . . . . . . . . . . . . . . . . . . . . . . . . . . . . . . . . . . .

Which part of this passage is particularly significant for you today?

# Day 18

Put yourself in Peter's place: in the pitch darkness, the wind buffeting the boat and the spray of the waves in your face. Jesus says to you, 'Come!' What would you do? What would you say?

. . . . . . . . . . . . . . . . . . . . . . . . . . . . . . . . . . . . . . . . . . . . . . . . . . . . . . . .

. . . . . . . . . . . . . . . . . . . . . . . . . . . . . . . . . . . . . . . . . . . . . . . . . . . . . . . .

. . . . . . . . . . . . . . . . . . . . . . . . . . . . . . . . . . . . . . . . . . . . . . . . . . . . . . . .

. . . . . . . . . . . . . . . . . . . . . . . . . . . . . . . . . . . . . . . . . . . . . . . . . . . . . . . .

. . . . . . . . . . . . . . . . . . . . . . . . . . . . . . . . . . . . . . . . . . . . . . . . . . . . . . . .

. . . . . . . . . . . . . . . . . . . . . . . . . . . . . . . . . . . . . . . . . . . . . . . . . . . . . . . .

. . . . . . . . . . . . . . . . . . . . . . . . . . . . . . . . . . . . . . . . . . . . . . .

Spend some time imagining yourself in this story. See what happens if you are brave enough to get out of the boat.

[13] When Jesus came to the region of Caesarea Philippi, he asked his disciples, 'Who do people say the Son of Man is?'
[14] They replied, 'Some say John the Baptist; others say Elijah; and still others, Jeremiah or one of the prophets.'
[15] 'But what about you?' he asked. 'Who do you say I am?'
[16] Simon Peter answered, 'You are the Messiah, the Son of the living God.'
[17] Jesus replied, 'Blessed are you, Simon son of Jonah, for this was not revealed to you by flesh and blood, but by my Father in heaven.

Matthew 16:13–17

# Day 19

Who is Jesus? A good moral teacher, a revolutionary who met a violent death, a historical figure who perhaps never even existed? Or the Messiah, the one in whom all God's purposes are fulfilled? This question is at the very core of the meaning of life. What is your answer?

## 'Jesus, I say that you are...

. . . . . . . . . . . . . . . . . . . . . . . . . . . . . . . . . . . . . . . . . . . . . . . . . . . . . . . . . .

. . . . . . . . . . . . . . . . . . . . . . . . . . . . . . . . . . . . . . . . . . . . . . . . . . . . . . . . . .

. . . . . . . . . . . . . . . . . . . . . . . . . . . . . . . . . . . . . . . . . . . . . . . . . . . . . . . . . .

. . . . . . . . . . . . . . . . . . . . . . . . . . . . . . . . . . . . . . . . . . . . . . . . . . . . . . . . . .

. . . . . . . . . . . . . . . . . . . . . . . . . . . . . . . . . . . . . . . . . . . . . . . . . . . . . . . . . .

. . . . . . . . . . . . . . . . . . . . . . . . . . . . . . . . . . . . . . . . . . . . . . . . . . . . . . . . . .

. . . . . . . . . . . . . . . . . . . . . . . . . . . . . . . . . . . . . . . . . . . . . . . . . . . . . . . . . .

. . . . . . . . . . . . . . . . . . . . . . . . . . . . . . . . . . . . . . . . . . . . . . . . . . . . . . . . . .

. . . . . . . . . . . . . . . . . . . . . . . . . . . . . . . . . . . . . . . . . . . . . . . . . . . . . . . . . .

. . . . . . . . . . . . . . . . . . . . . . . . . . . . . . . . . . . . . . . . . . . . . . . . . . . . . . . . . .

Spend some time with God asking him to reveal more of himself to you.

# Day 20

²¹ From that time on Jesus began to explain to his disciples that he must go to Jerusalem and suffer many things at the hands of the elders, the chief priests and the teachers of the law, and that he must be killed and on the third day be raised to life.

²² Peter took him aside and began to rebuke him. 'Never, Lord!' he said. 'This shall never happen to you!'

²³ Jesus turned and said to Peter, 'Get behind me, Satan! You are a stumbling-block to me; you do not have in mind the concerns of God, but merely human concerns.'

²⁴ Then Jesus said to his disciples, 'Whoever wants to be my disciple must deny themselves and take up their cross and follow me. ²⁵ For whoever wants to save their life will lose it, but whoever loses their life for me will find it. ²⁶ What good will it be for someone to gain the whole world, yet forfeit their soul? Or what can anyone give in exchange for their soul? ²⁷ For the Son of Man is going to come in his Father's glory with his angels, and then he will reward each person according to what they have done.

²⁸ 'Truly I tell you, some who are standing here will not taste death before they see the Son of Man coming in his kingdom.'

Matthew 16:21–28

# Day 20

Christianity is sometimes marketed attractively, sugar-coated to make it appeal to the widest possible audience. But we need to know what we are signing up to. Here, Jesus tells it as it is.

How do you react to Jesus' words to Peter in verse 23? Why did Jesus react so strongly?

. . . . . . . . . . . . . . . . . . . . . . . . . . . . . . . . . . . . . . . . . . . . . . .

. . . . . . . . . . . . . . . . . . . . . . . . . . . . . . . . . . . . . . . . . . . . . . .

. . . . . . . . . . . . . . . . . . . . . . . . . . . . . . . . . . . . . . . . . . . . . . .

. . . . . . . . . . . . . . . . . . . . . . . . . . . . . . . . . . . . . . . . . . . . . . .

. . . . . . . . . . . . . . . . . . . . . . . . . . . . . . . . . . . . . . . . . . . . . . .

. . . . . . . . . . . . . . . . . . . . . . . . . . . . . . . . . . . . . . . . . . . . . . .

. . . . . . . . . . . . . . . . . . . . . . . . . . . . . . . . . . . . . . . . . . . . . . .

. . . . . . . . . . . . . . . . . . . . . . . . . . . . . . . . . . . . . . . . . . . . . . .

. . . . . . . . . . . . . . . . . . . . . . . . . . . . . . . . . . . . . . . . . . . . . . .

. . . . . . . . . . . . . . . . . . . . . . . . . . . . . . . . . . . . . . . . . . . . . . .

. . . . . . . . . . . . . . . . . . . . . . . . . . . . . . . . . . . . . . . . . . . . . . .

. . . . . . . . . . . . . . . . . . . . . . . . . . . . . . . . . . . . . . . . . . . . . . .

. . . . . . . . . . . . . . . . . . . . . . . . . . . . . . . . . . . . . . . . . . .

# Day 20

'Deny yourself,' 'take up your cross,' 'lose your life' – these are huge demands. But what are the rewards? You will find life. We mustn't deceive ourselves: following Jesus is costly. It may well cost us everything. But what is the cost of not following him? What in the world could be more valuable?

Use the space to reflect on how you feel about this passage.

After six days Jesus took with him Peter, James and John
the brother of James, and led them up a high mountain by
themselves. ² There he was transfigured before them. His face
shone like the sun, and his clothes became as white as the light.
³ Just then there appeared before them Moses and Elijah, talking
with Jesus.

⁴ Peter said to Jesus, 'Lord, it is good for us to be here. If you
wish, I will put up three shelters – one for you, one for Moses
and one for Elijah.'

⁵ While he was still speaking, a bright cloud covered them, and a
voice from the cloud said, 'This is my Son, whom I love; with him
I am well pleased. Listen to him!'
⁶ When the disciples heard this, they fell face down to the
ground, terrified. ⁷ But Jesus came and touched them. 'Get up,'
he said. 'Don't be afraid.' ⁸ When they looked up, they saw no
one except Jesus.

Matthew 17:1–8

# Day 21

Jesus was conceived by an unmarried teenager, and yet his birth was announced by choirs of angels. He was born in a shed alongside animals, and yet he was there at creation. His closest friends were fishermen and yet he also keeps company with Old Testament legends Moses and Elijah. He burned with holiness and God himself confirmed his identity, and yet he was to be executed as a criminal in naked shame. Take some time to contemplate these paradoxical elements of who Jesus is.

. . . . . . . . . . . . . . . . . . . . . . . . . . . . . . . . . . . . . . . . .

. . . . . . . . . . . . . . . . . . . . . . . . . . . . . . . . . . . . . . . . .

. . . . . . . . . . . . . . . . . . . . . . . . . . . . . . . . . . . . . . . . .

. . . . . . . . . . . . . . . . . . . . . . . . . . . . . . . . . . . . . . . . .

. . . . . . . . . . . . . . . . . . . . . . . . . . . . . . . . . . . . . . . . .

. . . . . . . . . . . . . . . . . . . . . . . . . . . . . . . . . . . . . . . . .

. . . . . . . . . . . . . . . . . . . . . . . . . . . . . . . . . . . . . . . . .

. . . . . . . . . . . . . . . . . . . . . . . . . . . . . . . . . . . . . . . . .

. . . . . . . . . . . . . . . . . . . . . . . . . . . . . . . . . . . . . . . . .

. . . . . . . . . . . . . . . . . . . . . . . . . . . . . . . . . . . . . . . . .

. . . . . . . . . . . . . . . . . . . . . . . . . . . . . . . . . . . . . . . . .

. . . . . . . . . . . . . . . . . . . . . . . . . . . . . . . . . . . . . . . . .

The disciples' response to the voice from the cloud is to fall to the ground in terror (v 6). This was not an unusual reaction for someone to have in the presence of God. Jesus is 'the image of the invisible God' (Colossians 1:15), but he touches them, tells them to get up and calms their fear (v 7).

Have you had an experience of the overpowering presence of God? How did you respond?

. . . . . . . . . . . . . . . . . . . . . . . . . . . . . . . . . . . . . . . . . . . . . . . . . . . . . . . . . . . . . . . .

. . . . . . . . . . . . . . . . . . . . . . . . . . . . . . . . . . . . . . . . . . . . . . . . . . . . . . . . . . . . . . . .

. . . . . . . . . . . . . . . . . . . . . . . . . . . . . . . . . . . . . . . . . . . . . . . . . . . . . . . . . . . . . . . .

. . . . . . . . . . . . . . . . . . . . . . . . . . . . . . . . . . . . . . . . . . . . . . . . . . . . . . . . . . . . . . . .

. . . . . . . . . . . . . . . . . . . . . . . . . . . . . . . . . . . . . . . . . . . . . . . . . . . . . . . . . . . . . . . .

. . . . . . . . . . . . . . . . . . . . . . . . . . . . . . . . . . . . . . . . . . . . . . . . . . . . . . . .

Spend some time in God's presence. Listen for his voice.

# Day 22

At that time the disciples came to Jesus and asked, 'Who, then, is the greatest in the kingdom of heaven?'

² He called a little child to him, and placed the child among them. ³ And he said: 'Truly I tell you, unless you change and become like little children, you will never enter the kingdom of heaven. ⁴ Therefore, whoever takes the lowly position of this child is the greatest in the kingdom of heaven. ⁵ And whoever welcomes one such child in my name welcomes me.

Matthew 18:1–5

Jesus must've wanted to knock his disciples' heads together sometimes. They do so well, but then they ask him which of them is most important, a frequent argument. As usual, his answer turns things upside down.

Children were powerless in ancient society. They had no status or privilege other than that of their parents. What was Jesus saying about kingdom greatness when he told them to be like a child?

. . . . . . . . . . . . . . . . . . . . . . . . . . . . . . . . . . . . . . . . . . . . . . . . . . . . . . . . . . .

. . . . . . . . . . . . . . . . . . . . . . . . . . . . . . . . . . . . . . . . . . . . . . . . . . . . . . . . . . .

. . . . . . . . . . . . . . . . . . . . . . . . . . . . . . . . . . . . . . . . . . . . . . . . . . . . . . . . . . .

. . . . . . . . . . . . . . . . . . . . . . . . . . . . . . . . . . . . . . . . . . . . . . . . . . . . . . . . . . .

. . . . . . . . . . . . . . . . . . . . . . . . . . . . . . . . . . . . . . . . . . . . . . . . . . . . . . . . . . .

. . . . . . . . . . . . . . . . . . . . . . . . . . . . . . . . . . . . . . . . . . . . . . . . . . . . . . . . . . .

. . . . . . . . . . . . . . . . . . . . . . . . . . . . . . . . . . . . . . . . . . . . . . . . . . . . . . . . . . .

. . . . . . . . . . . . . . . . . . . . . . . . . . . . . . . . . . . . . . . . . . . . . . . . . . . . . . . . . . .

. . . . . . . . . . . . . . . . . . . . . . . . . . . . . . . . . . . . . . . . . . . . . . . . . . . . . . . . . . .

. . . . . . . . . . . . . . . . . . . . . . . . . . . . . . . . . . . . . . . . . . . .

# Day 22

The temptation to grab status and power for ourselves is very real, and something we all have to watch in ourselves. Meditate on Luke 22:26:

*'The greatest among you should be like the youngest, and the one who rules like the one who serves.'*

Ask God to help you seek greatness as he defines it, and not as it is defined by the world.

¹⁶ Just then a man came up to Jesus and asked, 'Teacher, what good thing must I do to get eternal life?'

¹⁷ 'Why do you ask me about what is good?' Jesus replied. 'There is only One who is good. If you want to enter life, keep the commandments.'

¹⁸ 'Which ones?' he enquired.

Jesus replied, '"You shall not murder, you shall not commit adultery, you shall not steal, you shall not give false testimony, ¹⁹ honour your father and mother,"[Ex 20:12–16] and "love your neighbour as yourself."[Lev 19:18]'

²⁰ 'All these I have kept,' the young man said. 'What do I still lack?'

²¹ Jesus answered, 'If you want to be perfect, go, sell your possessions and give to the poor, and you will have treasure in heaven. Then come, follow me.'

²² When the young man heard this, he went away sad, because he had great wealth.

²³ Then Jesus said to his disciples, 'Truly I tell you, it is hard for someone who is rich to enter the kingdom of heaven. ²⁴ Again I tell you, it is easier for a camel to go through the eye of a needle than for someone who is rich to enter the kingdom of God.'

²⁵ When the disciples heard this, they were greatly astonished and asked, 'Who then can be saved?'

²⁶ Jesus looked at them and said, 'With man this is impossible, but with God all things are possible.'

Matthew 19:16–26

# Day 23

Jesus is not pointlessly torturing this young man. He knows that he is a slave to his great wealth, and what he wants for him is freedom. Like the monkey with his hand stuck in a jar because he won't let go of the cookie, the man needs to let go of his possessions before he can truly worship God. What do you need to let go of?

. . . . . . . . . . . . . . . . . . . . . . . . . . . . . . . . . . . . . . . . . . . . . . .

. . . . . . . . . . . . . . . . . . . . . . . . . . . . . . . . . . . . . . . . . . . . . . .

. . . . . . . . . . . . . . . . . . . . . . . . . . . . . . . . . . . . . . . . . . . . . . .

. . . . . . . . . . . . . . . . . . . . . . . . . . . . . . . . . . . . . . . . . . . . . . .

. . . . . . . . . . . . . . . . . . . . . . . . . . . . . . . . . . . . . . . . . . . . . . .

. . . . . . . . . . . . . . . . . . . . . . . . . . . . . . . . . . . . . . . . . . . . . . .

. . . . . . . . . . . . . . . . . . . . . . . . . . . . . . . . . . . . . . . . . . . . . . .

. . . . . . . . . . . . . . . . . . . . . . . . . . . . . . . . . . . . . . . . . . . . . . .

. . . . . . . . . . . . . . . . . . . . . . . . . . . . . . . . . . . . . . . . . . . . . . .

. . . . . . . . . . . . . . . . . . . . . . . . . . . . . . . . . . . . . . . . . . . . . . .

. . . . . . . . . . . . . . . . . . . . . . . . . . . . . . . . . . . . . . . . . . . . . . .

. . . . . . . . . . . . . . . . . . . . . . . . . . . . . . . . . . . . . . . . . . . . . . .

If Jesus' words in verse 21 were addressed to you, how would you respond?

. . . . . . . . . . . . . . . . . . . . . . . . . . . . . . . . . . . . . . . . . . . . . . . . . . .

. . . . . . . . . . . . . . . . . . . . . . . . . . . . . . . . . . . . . . . . . . . . . . . . . . .

. . . . . . . . . . . . . . . . . . . . . . . . . . . . . . . . . . . . . . . . . . . . . . . . . . .

. . . . . . . . . . . . . . . . . . . . . . . . . . . . . . . . . . . . . . . . . . . . . . . . . . .

. . . . . . . . . . . . . . . . . . . . . . . . . . . . . . . . . . . . . . . . . . . . . . . . . . .

. . . . . . . . . . . . . . . . . . . . . . . . . . . . . . . . . . . . . . . . . . . . . . . . . . .

. . . . . . . . . . . . . . . . . . . . . . . . . . . . . . . . . . . . . . . . . . . . . . . . . . .

. . . . . . . . . . . . . . . . . . . . . . . . . . . . . . . . . . . . . . . . . . . . . . . . . . .

. . . . . . . . . . . . . . . . . . . . . . . . . . . . . . . . . . . . . . . . . . . . . . . . . . .

. . . . . . . . . . . . . . . . . . . . . . . . . . . . . . . . . . . . . . . . . . . . . . . . . . .

. . . . . . . . . . . . . . . . . . . . . . . . . . . . . . . . . . . . . . . . . . . . . . . . . . .

. . . . . . . . . . . . . . . . . . . . . . . . . . . . . . . . . . . . . . . . . . . . . . . . . . .

. . . . . . . . . . . . . . . . . . . . . . . . . . . . . . . . . . . . . . . . . . . . . . . . . . .

# Day 24

²⁹ As Jesus and his disciples were leaving Jericho, a large crowd followed him. ³⁰ Two blind men were sitting by the roadside, and when they heard that Jesus was passing by, they shouted, 'Lord, Son of David, have mercy on us!'

³¹ The crowd rebuked them and told them to be quiet, but they shouted all the louder, 'Lord, Son of David, have mercy on us!'

³² Jesus stopped and called them. 'What do you want me to do for you?' he asked.

³³ 'Lord,' they answered, 'we want our sight.'

³⁴ Jesus had compassion on them and touched their eyes. Immediately they received their sight and followed him.

Matthew 20:29–34

Imagine yourself sitting in the dust like the blind men. And then Jesus sees you. You have been noticed. How does that make you feel?

. . . . . . . . . . . . . . . . . . . . . . . . . . . . . . . . . . . . . . . . . . . . . . . . . . . . . . . . . . . . . . . . . . . . . . . . .

. . . . . . . . . . . . . . . . . . . . . . . . . . . . . . . . . . . . . . . . . . . . . . . . . . . . . . . . . . . . . . . . . . . . . . . . .

. . . . . . . . . . . . . . . . . . . . . . . . . . . . . . . . . . . . . . . . . . . . . . . . . . . . . . . . . . . . . . . . . . . . . . . . .

. . . . . . . . . . . . . . . . . . . . . . . . . . . . . . . . . . . . . . . . . . . . . . . . . . . . . . . . . . . . . . . . . . . . . . . . .

. . . . . . . . . . . . . . . . . . . . . . . . . . . . . . . . . . . . . . . . . . . . . . . . . . . . . . . . . . . . . . . . . . . . . . . . .

. . . . . . . . . . . . . . . . . . . . . . . . . . . . . . . . . . . . . . . . . . . . . . . . . . . . . . . . . . . . . . . . . . . . . . . . .

. . . . . . . . . . . . . . . . . . . . . . . . . . . . . . . . . . . . . . . . . . . . . . . . . . . . . . . . . . . . . . . . . . . . . . . . .

. . . . . . . . . . . . . . . . . . . . . . . . . . . . . . . . . . . . . . . . . . . . . . . . . . . . . . . . . . . . .

What does God want to say to you through this passage today?

# Day 24

What do you want from Jesus? Be brave, and ask him in prayer for the thing you most need right now. Use the space to note it down.

. . . . . . . . . . . . . . . . . . . . . . . . . . . . . . . . . . . . . . . . . . . . . . . . . . . . . . . . . . . . . . . . . . . . . . . . . . . . . . . . . . . .

. . . . . . . . . . . . . . . . . . . . . . . . . . . . . . . . . . . . . . . . . . . . . . . . . . . . . . . . . . . . . . . . . . . . . . . . . . . . . . . . . . . .

. . . . . . . . . . . . . . . . . . . . . . . . . . . . . . . . . . . . . . . . . . . . . . . . . . . . . . . . . . . . . . . . . . . . . . . . . . . . . . . . . . . .

. . . . . . . . . . . . . . . . . . . . . . . . . . . . . . . . . . . . . . . . . . . . . . . . . . . . . . . . . . . . . . . . . . . . . . . . . . . . . . . . . . . .

. . . . . . . . . . . . . . . . . . . . . . . . . . . . . . . . . . . . . . . . . . . . . . . . . . . . . . . . . . . . . . . . . . . . . . . . . . . . . . . . . . . .

. . . . . . . . . . . . . . . . . . . . . . . . . . . . . . . . . . . . . . . . . . . . . . . . . . . . . . . . . . . . . . . . . . . . . . . . . . . . . . . . . . . .

. . . . . . . . . . . . . . . . . . . . . . . . . . . . . . . . . . . . . . . . . . . . . . . . . . . . . . . . . . . . . . . . . . . . . . . . . . . . . . . . . . . .

. . . . . . . . . . . . . . . . . . . . . . . . . . . . . . . . . . . . . . . . . . . . . . . . . . . . . . . . . . . . . . . . . . . . . . .

As they approached Jerusalem and came to Bethphage on the Mount of Olives, Jesus sent two disciples, [2] saying to them, 'Go to the village ahead of you, and at once you will find a donkey tied there, with her colt by her. Untie them and bring them to me. [3] If anyone says anything to you, say that the Lord needs them, and he will send them right away.'

[4] This took place to fulfil what was spoken through the prophet:

[5] 'Say to Daughter Zion,
    "See, your king comes to you,
gentle and riding on a donkey,
    and on a colt, the foal of a donkey."' [Zech 9:9]

[6] The disciples went and did as Jesus had instructed them. [7] They brought the donkey and the colt and placed their cloaks on them for Jesus to sit on. [8] A very large crowd spread their cloaks on the road, while others cut branches from the trees and spread them on the road. [9] The crowds that went ahead of him and those that followed shouted,

'Hosanna to the Son of David!'

'Blessed is he who comes in the name of the Lord!' [Ps 118:25,26]

'Hosanna in the highest heaven!'

[10] When Jesus entered Jerusalem, the whole city was stirred and asked, 'Who is this?'

[11] The crowds answered, 'This is Jesus, the prophet from Nazareth in Galilee.'

Matthew 21:1–11

# Day 25

Which part of this passage particularly strikes you?

. . . . . . . . . . . . . . . . . . . . . . . . . . . . . . . . . . . . . . . . . . . . . .

. . . . . . . . . . . . . . . . . . . . . . . . . . . . . . . . . . . . . . . . . . . . . .

. . . . . . . . . . . . . . . . . . . . . . . . . . . . . . . . . . . . . . . . . . . . . .

. . . . . . . . . . . . . . . . . . . . . . . . . . . . . . . . . . . . . . . . . . . . . .

. . . . . . . . . . . . . . . . . . . . . . . . . . . . . . . . . . . . . . . . . . . . . .

. . . . . . . . . . . . . . . . . . . . . . . . . . . . . . . . . . . . . . . . . . . . . .

. . . . . . . . . . . . . . . . . . . . . . . . . . . . . . . . . . . . . . . . . . . . . .

. . . . . . . . . . . . . . . . . . . . . . . . . . . . . . . . . . . . . . .

What does God want to say to you through this passage?

. . . . . . . . . . . . . . . . . . . . . . . . . . . . . . . . . . . . . . . . . . . . . .

. . . . . . . . . . . . . . . . . . . . . . . . . . . . . . . . . . . . . . . . . . . . . .

. . . . . . . . . . . . . . . . . . . . . . . . . . . . . . . . . . . . . . . . . . . . . .

. . . . . . . . . . . . . . . . . . . . . . . . . . . . . . . . . . . . . . . . . . . . . .

. . . . . . . . . . . . . . . . . . . . . . . . . . . . . . . . . . . . . . . . . . . . . .

. . . . . . . . . . . . . . . . . . . . . . . . . . . . . . . . . . . . . . . . . . . . . .

. . . . . . . . . . . . . . . . . . . . . . . . . . . . . . . . . . . . . . . . . . . . . .

. . . . . . . . . . . . . . . . . . . . . . . . . . . . . . . . . . . . . . . . . . . . . .

. . . . . . . . . . . . . . . . . . . . . . . . . . . . . . . . . . . . . . .

# Day 25

There was a mismatch between the kind of king the crowds wanted and expected Jesus to be, and the kind of king that he was. What has surprised or challenged you about the Jesus you have come to know through your readings in Matthew so far?

# Day 26

[34] Hearing that Jesus had silenced the Sadducees, the Pharisees got together. [35] One of them, an expert in the law, tested him with this question: [36] 'Teacher, which is the greatest commandment in the Law?'

[37] Jesus replied: '"Love the Lord your God with all your heart and with all your soul and with all your mind."[Deut 6:5] [38] This is the first and greatest commandment. [39] And the second is like it: "Love your neighbour as yourself."[Lev 19:18] [40] All the Law and the Prophets hang on these two commandments.'

Matthew 22:34–40

# Day 26

There were 613 commandments in the Law. Why did Jesus choose these two as the greatest?

. . . . . . . . . . . . . . . . . . . . . . . . . . . . . . . . . . . . . . . . . . . . . . . . . . . . . . . . .

. . . . . . . . . . . . . . . . . . . . . . . . . . . . . . . . . . . . . . . . . . . . . . . . . . . . . . . . .

. . . . . . . . . . . . . . . . . . . . . . . . . . . . . . . . . . . . . . . . . . . . . . . . . . . . . . . . .

. . . . . . . . . . . . . . . . . . . . . . . . . . . . . . . . . . . . . . . . . . . . . . . . . . . . . . . . .

. . . . . . . . . . . . . . . . . . . . . . . . . . . . . . . . . . . . . . . . . . . . . . . . . . . . . . . . .

. . . . . . . . . . . . . . . . . . . . . . . . . . . . . . . . . . . . . . . . . . . . . . . . . . . . . . . . .

. . . . . . . . . . . . . . . . . . . . . . . . . . . . . . . . . . . . . . . . . . . . . .

What does it mean for us to love God with heart, soul and mind?

# Day 26

Sometimes religion is associated with rules and restrictions. How does it change things if you start with love of God and others?

. . . . . . . . . . . . . . . . . . . . . . . . . . . . . . . . . . . . . . . . . . . . . . . . . . . . . . . . .

. . . . . . . . . . . . . . . . . . . . . . . . . . . . . . . . . . . . . . . . . . . . . . . . . . . . . . . . .

. . . . . . . . . . . . . . . . . . . . . . . . . . . . . . . . . . . . . . . . . . . . . . . . . . . . . . . . .

. . . . . . . . . . . . . . . . . . . . . . . . . . . . . . . . . . . . . . . . . . . . . . . . . . . . . . . . .

. . . . . . . . . . . . . . . . . . . . . . . . . . . . . . . . . . . . . . . . . . . . . . . . . . . . . . . . .

. . . . . . . . . . . . . . . . . . . . . . . . . . . . . . . . . . . . . . . . . . . . . . . . . .

Ask God to expand your understanding of his love for you.
Let the Spirit speak the truth of his love into the core of who you are.

'At that time the kingdom of heaven will be like ten virgins who took their lamps and went out to meet the bridegroom. [2] Five of them were foolish and five were wise. [3] The foolish ones took their lamps but did not take any oil with them. [4] The wise ones, however, took oil in jars along with their lamps. [5] The bridegroom was a long time in coming, and they all became drowsy and fell asleep.

[6] 'At midnight the cry rang out: "Here's the bridegroom! Come out to meet him!"

[7] 'Then all the virgins woke up and trimmed their lamps. [8] The foolish ones said to the wise, "Give us some of your oil; our lamps are going out."

[9] '"No," they replied, "there may not be enough for both us and you. Instead, go to those who sell oil and buy some for yourselves."

[10] 'But while they were on their way to buy the oil, the bridegroom arrived. The virgins who were ready went in with him to the wedding banquet. And the door was shut.

[11] 'Later the others also came. "Lord, Lord," they said, "open the door for us!"

[12] 'But he replied, "Truly I tell you, I don't know you."

[13] 'Therefore keep watch, because you do not know the day or the hour.

Matthew 25:1–13

# Day 27

The Jews had been waiting for the Messiah for generations (v 5), but many of them weren't ready to respond when he arrived (v 10).

What can you learn from this passage about God's timing?

. . . . . . . . . . . . . . . . . . . . . . . . . . . . . . . . . . . . . . . . . . . . . . . . . . . . . . . . . .

. . . . . . . . . . . . . . . . . . . . . . . . . . . . . . . . . . . . . . . . . . . . . . . . . . . . . . . . . .

. . . . . . . . . . . . . . . . . . . . . . . . . . . . . . . . . . . . . . . . . . . . . . . . . . . . . . . . . .

. . . . . . . . . . . . . . . . . . . . . . . . . . . . . . . . . . . . . . . . . . . . . . . . . . . . . . . . . .

. . . . . . . . . . . . . . . . . . . . . . . . . . . . . . . . . . . . . . . . . . . . . . . . . . . . . . . . . .

. . . . . . . . . . . . . . . . . . . . . . . . . . . . . . . . . . . . . . . . . . . . . . . . . . . . . . . . . .

. . . . . . . . . . . . . . . . . . . . . . . . . . . . . . . . . . . . . . . . . . . . . . . . . . .

How does the idea of Jesus returning again make you feel?

# Day 27

We are in a period of waiting again, waiting for Jesus to return: 'When the Son of Man comes in his glory, and all the angels with him, he will sit on his glorious throne … and he will separate the people one from another as a shepherd separates the sheep from the goats' (Matthew 25:31,32).

How can we make sure we are ready for Jesus' return?

¹⁷ On the first day of the Festival of Unleavened Bread, the disciples came to Jesus and asked, 'Where do you want us to make preparations for you to eat the Passover?'

¹⁸ He replied, 'Go into the city to a certain man and tell him, "The Teacher says: my appointed time is near. I am going to celebrate the Passover with my disciples at your house."'
¹⁹ So the disciples did as Jesus had directed them and prepared the Passover.

²⁰ When evening came, Jesus was reclining at the table with the Twelve. ²¹ And while they were eating, he said, 'Truly I tell you, one of you will betray me.'

²² They were very sad and began to say to him one after the other, 'Surely you don't mean me, Lord?'

²³ Jesus replied, 'The one who has dipped his hand into the bowl with me will betray me. ²⁴ The Son of Man will go just as it is written about him. But woe to that man who betrays the Son of Man! It would be better for him if he had not been born.'

²⁵ Then Judas, the one who would betray him, said, 'Surely you don't mean me, Rabbi?'

Jesus answered, 'You have said so.'

²⁶ While they were eating, Jesus took bread, and when he had given thanks, he broke it and gave it to his disciples, saying, 'Take and eat; this is my body.'

²⁷ Then he took a cup, and when he had given thanks, he gave it to them, saying, 'Drink from it, all of you.
²⁸ This is my blood of the covenant, which is poured out for many for the forgiveness of sins. ²⁹ I tell you, I will not drink from this fruit of the vine from now on until that day when I drink it new with you in my Father's kingdom.'

Matthew 26:17–29

Christians around the world still drink wine and eat bread in remembrance of what Jesus did. As with any ritual, it is easy to lose the impact of its significance with time and familiarity. Allow yourself to be shocked by the words – 'drink my blood', 'eat my flesh'. The next time you take communion, make a special effort to engage with its meaning.

What does drinking wine and eating bread in remembrance of Jesus mean to you?

. . . . . . . . . . . . . . . . . . . . . . . . . . . . . . . . . . . . . . . . . . . . . . . .

. . . . . . . . . . . . . . . . . . . . . . . . . . . . . . . . . . . . . . . . . . . . . . . .

. . . . . . . . . . . . . . . . . . . . . . . . . . . . . . . . . . . . . . . . . . . . . . . .

. . . . . . . . . . . . . . . . . . . . . . . . . . . . . . . . . . . . . . . . . . . . . . . .

. . . . . . . . . . . . . . . . . . . . . . . . . . . . . . . . . . . . . . . . . . . . . . . .

. . . . . . . . . . . . . . . . . . . . . . . . . . . . . . . . . . . . . . . . . . . . . . . .

. . . . . . . . . . . . . . . . . . . . . . . . . . . . . . . . . . . . . . . . . . . . . . . .

. . . . . . . . . . . . . . . . . . . . . . . . . . . . . . . . . . . . . . . . . . . . . . . .

. . . . . . . . . . . . . . . . . . . . . . . . . . . . . . . . . . . . . . . . . . . . . . . .

. . . . . . . . . . . . . . . . . . . . . . . . . . . . . . . . . . . . . . . . . . . . . . . .

. . . . . . . . . . . . . . . . . . . . . . . . . . . . . . . . . . . . . . . . . . . . . . . .

. . . . . . . . . . . . . . . . . . . . . . . . . . . . . . . . . . . . . . . . . .

Jesus gives new meaning to the familiar symbols of Passover: he is the lamb to be slain (Exodus 12) for the salvation of many.

# Day 28

We might be horrified by Judas' actions, but who hasn't betrayed Jesus in big or small ways? Take time to say sorry to Jesus, and thank him for his faithfulness and mercy: **'while we were still sinners, Christ died for us'** (Romans 5:8).

³⁶ Then Jesus went with his disciples to a place called Gethsemane, and he said to them, 'Sit here while I go over there and pray.' ³⁷ He took Peter and the two sons of Zebedee along with him, and he began to be sorrowful and troubled. ³⁸ Then he said to them, 'My soul is overwhelmed with sorrow to the point of death. Stay here and keep watch with me.'

³⁹ Going a little farther, he fell with his face to the ground and prayed, 'My Father, if it is possible, may this cup be taken from me. Yet not as I will, but as you will.'

⁴⁰ Then he returned to his disciples and found them sleeping. 'Couldn't you men keep watch with me for one hour?' he asked Peter. ⁴¹ 'Watch and pray so that you will not fall into temptation. The spirit is willing, but the flesh is weak.'

⁴² He went away a second time and prayed, 'My Father, if it is not possible for this cup to be taken away unless I drink it, may your will be done.'

⁴³ When he came back, he again found them sleeping, because their eyes were heavy. ⁴⁴ So he left them and went away once more and prayed the third time, saying the same thing.

⁴⁵ Then he returned to the disciples and said to them, 'Are you still sleeping and resting? Look, the hour has come, and the Son of Man is delivered into the hands of sinners. ⁴⁶ Rise! Let us go! Here comes my betrayer!'

Matthew 26:36–46

# Day 29

To understand Jesus, we have to grasp both his divinity and his humanity. It is here, in Gethsemane, that we see him at his most vulnerable, facing what is coming and pleading for another way out.

Jesus has been to the blackest place a person can go. He has experienced betrayal, sorrow, temptation, desperation, pain – and he knows exactly how you feel at your worst.

Be honest with him about your darkest times.

. . . . . . . . . . . . . . . . . . . . . . . . . . . . . . . . . . . . . . . . . . . . . . . . .

. . . . . . . . . . . . . . . . . . . . . . . . . . . . . . . . . . . . . . . . . . . . . . . . .

. . . . . . . . . . . . . . . . . . . . . . . . . . . . . . . . . . . . . . . . . . . . . . . . .

. . . . . . . . . . . . . . . . . . . . . . . . . . . . . . . . . . . . . . . . . . . . . . . . .

. . . . . . . . . . . . . . . . . . . . . . . . . . . . . . . . . . . . . . . . . . . . . . . . .

. . . . . . . . . . . . . . . . . . . . . . . . . . . . . . . . . . . . . . . . . . . . . . . . .

. . . . . . . . . . . . . . . . . . . . . . . . . . . . . . . . . . . . . . . . . . . . . . . . .

. . . . . . . . . . . . . . . . . . . . . . . . . . . . . . . . . . . . . . . . . . . . . . . . .

. . . . . . . . . . . . . . . . . . . . . . . . . . . . . . . . . . . . . . . . . . . . . . . . .

. . . . . . . . . . . . . . . . . . . . . . . . . . . . . . . . . . . . . . . . . . . . . . . . .

. . . . . . . . . . . . . . . . . . . . . . . . . . . . . . . . . . . . . . . . . . . . . . . . .

. . . . . . . . . . . . . . . . . . . . . . . . . . . . . . . . . . . . . . . . . . . . . . . . .

. . . . . . . . . . . . . . . . . . . . . . . . . . . . . . . . . . . . . . . . . . . .

Is there a situation in your life when you can see what the right thing to do is but it seems too hard? Ask God for the courage to echo Jesus' words, **'Not as I will, but as you will'** (v 39).

How does this insight into what this sacrifice cost Jesus affect how you receive the gift of his grace?

# Day 30

⁴⁷ While he was still speaking, Judas, one of the Twelve, arrived. With him was a large crowd armed with swords and clubs, sent from the chief priests and the elders of the people. ⁴⁸ Now the betrayer had arranged a signal with them: 'The one I kiss is the man; arrest him.'

⁴⁹ Going at once to Jesus, Judas said, 'Greetings, Rabbi!' and kissed him.

⁵⁰ Jesus replied, 'Do what you came for, friend.'

Then the men stepped forward, seized Jesus and arrested him. ⁵¹ With that, one of Jesus' companions reached for his sword, drew it out and struck the servant of the high priest, cutting off his ear.

⁵² 'Put your sword back in its place,' Jesus said to him, 'for all who draw the sword will die by the sword. ⁵³ Do you think I cannot call on my Father, and he will at once put at my disposal more than twelve legions of angels? ⁵⁴ But how then would the Scriptures be fulfilled that say it must happen in this way?'

⁵⁵ In that hour Jesus said to the crowd, 'Am I leading a rebellion, that you have come out with swords and clubs to capture me? Every day I sat in the temple courts teaching, and you did not arrest me. ⁵⁶ But this has all taken place that the writings of the prophets might be fulfilled.' Then all the disciples deserted him and fled.

Matthew 26:47–56

# Day 30

Is there anyone in your life who has betrayed you?
How do you feel about them now?

Talk to Jesus about how you feel. Listen for his response.

. . . . . . . . . . . . . . . . . . . . . . . . . . . . . . . . . . . . . . . . . . . . . . . . .

. . . . . . . . . . . . . . . . . . . . . . . . . . . . . . . . . . . . . . . . . . . . . . . .

. . . . . . . . . . . . . . . . . . . . . . . . . . . . . . . . . . . . . . . . . . . . . . . .

. . . . . . . . . . . . . . . . . . . . . . . . . . . . . . . . . . . . . . . . . . . . . . . . .

. . . . . . . . . . . . . . . . . . . . . . . . . . . . . . . . . . . . . . . . . . . . . . .

. . . . . . . . . . . . . . . . . . . . . . . . . . . . . . . . . . . . . . . . . . . . . . . .

. . . . . . . . . . . . . . . . . . . . . . . . . . . . . . . . . . . . . . . . . . . . . . .

. . . . . . . . . . . . . . . . . . . . . . . . . . . . . . . . . . . . . . . . . . . . . . .

. . . . . . . . . . . . . . . . . . . . . . . . . . . . . . . . . . . . . . . . . . . . . . .

. . . . . . . . . . . . . . . . . . . . . . . . . . . . . . . . . . . . . . . . . . . . . . .

. . . . . . . . . . . . . . . . . . . . . . . . . . . . . . . . . . . . . . . . . . . . . . .

. . . . . . . . . . . . . . . . . . . . . . . . . . . . . . . . . . .

○○○○○○○○○○○○○○○○○○○○○○○○○○○○○●○○○○○○○○○○

# Day 30

Jesus knows the Scriptures inside out, and they give him strength, courage and purpose (vs 54,56). How can you ensure that the Bible is a source of help when life is hard?

...............................................................................

...............................................................................

...............................................................................

...............................................................................

...............................................................................

...............................................................................

...............................................................................

'Jesus, help me to become more like you as I get to know you.'

⁵⁷ Those who had arrested Jesus took him to Caiaphas the high priest, where the teachers of the law and the elders had assembled. ⁵⁸ But Peter followed him at a distance, right up to the courtyard of the high priest. He entered and sat down with the guards to see the outcome.

⁵⁹ The chief priests and the whole Sanhedrin were looking for false evidence against Jesus so that they could put him to death. ⁶⁰ But they did not find any, though many false witnesses came forward.

Finally two came forward ⁶¹ and declared, 'This fellow said, "I am able to destroy the temple of God and rebuild it in three days."'

⁶² Then the high priest stood up and said to Jesus, 'Are you not going to answer? What is this testimony that these men are bringing against you?' ⁶³ But Jesus remained silent.

The high priest said to him, 'I charge you under oath by the living God: Tell us if you are the Messiah, the Son of God.'

⁶⁴ 'You have said so,' Jesus replied. 'But I say to all of you: from now on you will see the Son of Man sitting at the right hand of the Mighty One and coming on the clouds of heaven.'
[Ps 110:1, Dan 7:13]

⁶⁵ Then the high priest tore his clothes and said, 'He has spoken blasphemy! Why do we need any more witnesses? Look, now you have heard the blasphemy.
⁶⁶ What do you think?'

'He is worthy of death,' they answered.

⁶⁷ Then they spat in his face and struck him with their fists. Others slapped him ⁶⁸ and said, 'Prophesy to us, Messiah. Who hit you?'

Matthew 26:57–68

# Day 31

Imagine the scene described in this passage.

What do you notice?

How do you feel?

What do you want to say to God?

. . . . . . . . . . . . . . . . . . . . . . . . . . . . . . . . . . . . . . . . . . . . . . . . . . . . . . . . . . . . . . . . . . . . . .

. . . . . . . . . . . . . . . . . . . . . . . . . . . . . . . . . . . . . . . . . . . . . . . . . . . . . . . . . . . . . . . . . . . . . .

. . . . . . . . . . . . . . . . . . . . . . . . . . . . . . . . . . . . . . . . . . . . . . . . . . . . . . . . . . . . . . . . . . . . . .

. . . . . . . . . . . . . . . . . . . . . . . . . . . . . . . . . . . . . . . . . . . . . . . . . . . . . . . . . . . . . . . . . . . . . .

. . . . . . . . . . . . . . . . . . . . . . . . . . . . . . . . . . . . . . . . . . . . . . . . . . . . . . . . . . . . . . . . . . . . . .

. . . . . . . . . . . . . . . . . . . . . . . . . . . . . . . . . . . . . . . . . . . . . . . . . . . . . . . . . . . . . . . . . . . . . .

. . . . . . . . . . . . . . . . . . . . . . . . . . . . . . . . . . . . . . . . . . . . . . . . . . . . . . . . . . . . . . . . . . . . . .

. . . . . . . . . . . . . . . . . . . . . . . . . . . . . . . . . . . . . . . . . . . . . . . . . . . . . . . . . . . . . . . . . . . . . .

# Day 31

Spend some time reflecting on these two pictures of
Jesus, one glorified and exalted, the other beaten and
despised. This is our God.

........................................................

........................................................

........................................................

........................................................

........................................................

........................................................

........................................................

........................................................

........................................................

........................................................

........................................................

........................................................

........................................................

........................................................

........................................................

........................................................

........................................................

# Day 32

[69] Now Peter was sitting out in the courtyard, and a servant-girl came to him. 'You also were with Jesus of Galilee,' she said.

[70] But he denied it before them all. 'I don't know what you're talking about,' he said.

[71] Then he went out to the gateway, where another servant-girl saw him and said to the people there, 'This fellow was with Jesus of Nazareth.'

[72] He denied it again, with an oath: 'I don't know the man!'

[73] After a little while, those standing there went up to Peter and said, 'Surely you are one of them; your accent gives you away.'

[74] Then he began to call down curses, and he swore to them, 'I don't know the man!'

Immediately a cock crowed. [75] Then Peter remembered the word Jesus had spoken: 'Before the cock crows, you will disown me three times.' And he went outside and wept bitterly.

Matthew 26:69–75

# Day 32

There are all sorts of ways to cry – softly and sadly, great heaving sobs of self-pity, secretive snuffles, hot, angry tears... Peter, Matthew tells us, 'wept bitterly'. Why?

When was the last time you shed a tear? Talk with Jesus about your emotions.

. . . . . . . . . . . . . . . . . . . . . . . . . . . . . . . . . . . . . . . . . . . . . . . . . . . . . . . . .

. . . . . . . . . . . . . . . . . . . . . . . . . . . . . . . . . . . . . . . . . . . . . . . . . . . . . . . . .

. . . . . . . . . . . . . . . . . . . . . . . . . . . . . . . . . . . . . . . . . . . . . . . . . . . . . . . . .

. . . . . . . . . . . . . . . . . . . . . . . . . . . . . . . . . . . . . . . . . . . . . . . . . . . . . . . . .

. . . . . . . . . . . . . . . . . . . . . . . . . . . . . . . . . . . . . . . . . . . . . . . . . . . . . . . . .

. . . . . . . . . . . . . . . . . . . . . . . . . . . . . . . . . . . . . . . . . . . . . . . . . . . . . . . . .

. . . . . . . . . . . . . . . . . . . . . . . . . . . . . . . . . . . . . . . . . . . . . . . . . . . . . . . . .

. . . . . . . . . . . . . . . . . . . . . . . . . . . . . . . . . . . . . . . . . . . . . . . .

Jesus had predicted Peter's denials, down to the detail of the cockerel's crow. If Peter needed any more evidence that Jesus was who he said he was, he had it.

# Day 32

We have all let Jesus down at times. Pray for the courage to acknowledge that you are 'one of them', whatever the consequences. Ask God to forgive you for being less than you want to be, and thank him that he loves you anyway.

. . . . . . . . . . . . . . . . . . . . . . . . . . . . . . . . . . . . . . . . . . . . . .

. . . . . . . . . . . . . . . . . . . . . . . . . . . . . . . . . . . . . . . . . . . . . .

. . . . . . . . . . . . . . . . . . . . . . . . . . . . . . . . . . . . . . . . . . . . . .

. . . . . . . . . . . . . . . . . . . . . . . . . . . . . . . . . . . . . . . . . . . . . .

. . . . . . . . . . . . . . . . . . . . . . . . . . . . . . . . . . . . . . . . . . . . . .

. . . . . . . . . . . . . . . . . . . . . . . . . . . . . . . . . . . . . . . . . . . . . .

. . . . . . . . . . . . . . . . . . . . . . . . . . . . . . . . . . . . . . . . . . . . . .

. . . . . . . . . . . . . . . . . . . . . . . . . . . . . . . . . . . . . . . . . . . . . .

. . . . . . . . . . . . . . . . . . . . . . . . . . . . . . . . . . . . . . . . . . . . . .

. . . . . . . . . . . . . . . . . . . . . . . . . . . . . . . . . . . . . . . . . . . . . .

. . . . . . . . . . . . . . . . . . . . . . . . . . . . . . . . . . . . . . . . . . . . . .

. . . . . . . . . . . . . . . . . . . . . . . . . . . . . . . . . . . . . . . . . . . . . .

. . . . . . . . . . . . . . . . . . . . . . . . . . . . . . . . . . . . . . . . . . . . . .

. . . . . . . . . . . . . . . . . . . . . . . . . . . . . . . . . . . . . . . . . . . . . .

. . . . . . . . . . . . . . . . . . . . . . . . . . . . . . . . . . . . . . . . . . . . . .

. . . . . . . . . . . . . . . . . . . . . . . . . . . .

<sup>11</sup> Meanwhile Jesus stood before the governor, and the governor asked him, 'Are you the king of the Jews?'

'You have said so,' Jesus replied.

<sup>12</sup> When he was accused by the chief priests and the elders, he gave no answer.
<sup>13</sup> Then Pilate asked him, 'Don't you hear the testimony they are bringing against you?'
<sup>14</sup> But Jesus made no reply, not even to a single charge – to the great amazement of the governor.

<sup>15</sup> Now it was the governor's custom at the festival to release a prisoner chosen by the crowd. <sup>16</sup> At that time they had a well-known prisoner whose name was Jesus Barabbas.
<sup>17</sup> So when the crowd had gathered, Pilate asked them, 'Which one do you want me to release to you: Jesus Barabbas, or Jesus who is called the Messiah?' <sup>18</sup> For he knew it was out of self-interest that they had handed Jesus over to him.

<sup>19</sup> While Pilate was sitting on the judge's seat, his wife sent him this message: 'Don't have anything to do with that innocent man, for I have suffered a great deal today in a dream because of him.'

<sup>20</sup> But the chief priests and the elders persuaded the crowd to ask for Barabbas and to have Jesus executed.

<sup>21</sup> 'Which of the two do you want me to release to you?' asked the governor.

'Barabbas,' they answered.

<sup>22</sup> 'What shall I do, then, with Jesus who is called the Messiah?' Pilate asked.

They all answered, 'Crucify him!'

<sup>23</sup> 'Why? What crime has he committed?' asked Pilate.

But they shouted all the louder, 'Crucify him!'

<sup>24</sup> When Pilate saw that he was getting nowhere, but that instead an uproar was starting, he took water and washed his hands in front of the crowd. 'I am innocent of this man's blood,' he said. 'It is your responsibility!'

<sup>25</sup> All the people answered, 'His blood is on us and on our children!'

<sup>26</sup> Then he released Barabbas to them. But he had Jesus flogged, and handed him over to be crucified.

Matthew 27:11–26

# Day 33

It was all part of God's plan.
Re-read this passage and then turn to John 3:16.

What stands out to you?

What do you want to say to God?

What does God want to say to you?

# Day 33

We are all implicated in the death of Jesus. Read these words from Isaiah slowly and prayerfully, and try to absorb what the death of Jesus means for all of us:

'Surely he took up our pain and bore our suffering,
yet we considered him punished by God, stricken
by him, and afflicted. But he was pierced for our
transgressions, he was crushed for our iniquities; the
punishment that brought us peace was on him, and by
his wounds we are healed' (Isaiah 53:4–6).

. . . . . . . . . . . . . . . . . . . . . . . . . . . . . . . . . . . . . . . . . . . . . . . . . . . . . . . . . .

. . . . . . . . . . . . . . . . . . . . . . . . . . . . . . . . . . . . . . . . . . . . . . . . . . . . . . . . . .

. . . . . . . . . . . . . . . . . . . . . . . . . . . . . . . . . . . . . . . . . . . . . . . . . . . . . . . . . .

. . . . . . . . . . . . . . . . . . . . . . . . . . . . . . . . . . . . . . . . . . . . . . . . . . . . . . . . . .

. . . . . . . . . . . . . . . . . . . . . . . . . . . . . . . . . . . . . . . . . . . . . . . . . . . . . . . . . .

. . . . . . . . . . . . . . . . . . . . . . . . . . . . . . . . . . . . . . . . . . . . . . . . . . . . . . . . . .

. . . . . . . . . . . . . . . . . . . . . . . . . . . . . . . . . . . . . . . . . . . . . . . . . . . . . . . . . .

# Day 34

²⁷ Then the governor's soldiers took Jesus into the Praetorium and gathered the whole company of soldiers round him. ²⁸ They stripped him and put a scarlet robe on him, ²⁹ and then twisted together a crown of thorns and set it on his head. They put a staff in his right hand. Then they knelt in front of him and mocked him. 'Hail, king of the Jews!' they said. ³⁰ They spat on him, and took the staff and struck him on the head again and again. ³¹ After they had mocked him, they took off the robe and put his own clothes on him. Then they led him away to crucify him.

Matthew 27:27–31

The Jews wanted Jesus to be a leader who could deliver them from their political oppressors. It was clear at this moment that this was not what Jesus had come to do.

Whose voices still mock Jesus today?

What can you do to help others understand who Jesus really is?

# Day 34

This is a brutal account of bullying and torture. What situations are you aware of in the world at the moment where the strong are abusing power?

How can you stand up for justice?

. . . . . . . . . . . . . . . . . . . . . . . . . . . . . . . . . . . . . . . . . . . . . . . . . . . . . . . . . . . . . . . . . . . . .

. . . . . . . . . . . . . . . . . . . . . . . . . . . . . . . . . . . . . . . . . . . . . . . . . . . . . . . . . . . . . . . . . . . . .

. . . . . . . . . . . . . . . . . . . . . . . . . . . . . . . . . . . . . . . . . . . . . . . . . . . . . . . . . . . . . . . . . . . . .

. . . . . . . . . . . . . . . . . . . . . . . . . . . . . . . . . . . . . . . . . . . . . . . . . . . . . . . . . . . . . . . . . . . . .

. . . . . . . . . . . . . . . . . . . . . . . . . . . . . . . . . . . . . . . . . . . . . . . . . . . . . . . . . . . . . . . . . . . . .

. . . . . . . . . . . . . . . . . . . . . . . . . . . . . . . . . . . . . . . . . . . . . . . . . . . . . . . . . . . . . . . . . . . . .

. . . . . . . . . . . . . . . . . . . . . . . . . . . . . . . . . . . . . . . . . . . . . . . . . . . . . . . . . . .

'Jesus, you are my King. I kneel before you and worship you now.'

<sup>32</sup> As they were going out, they met a man from Cyrene, named Simon, and they forced him to carry the cross. <sup>33</sup> They came to a place called Golgotha (which means 'the place of the skull'). <sup>34</sup> There they offered Jesus wine to drink, mixed with gall; but after tasting it, he refused to drink it. <sup>35</sup> When they had crucified him, they divided up his clothes by casting lots. <sup>36</sup> And sitting down, they kept watch over him there. <sup>37</sup> Above his head they placed the written charge against him: THIS IS JESUS, THE KING OF THE JEWS.

<sup>38</sup> Two rebels were crucified with him, one on his right and one on his left. <sup>39</sup> Those who passed by hurled insults at him, shaking their heads <sup>40</sup> and saying, 'You who are going to destroy the temple and build it in three days, save yourself! Come down from the cross, if you are the Son of God!' <sup>41</sup> In the same way the chief priests, the teachers of the law and the elders mocked him. <sup>42</sup> 'He saved others,' they said, 'but he can't save himself! He's the king of Israel! Let him come down now from the cross, and we will believe in him. <sup>43</sup> He trusts in God. Let God rescue him now if he wants him, for he said, "I am the Son of God."' <sup>44</sup> In the same way the rebels who were crucified with him also heaped insults on him.

Matthew 27:32–44

# Day 35

Compare Matthew's account of Jesus' crucifixion with these words from Psalm 22, written centuries earlier:

**'All who see me mock me; they hurl insults, shaking their heads. "He trusts in the LORD," they say, "let the LORD rescue him."... a pack of villains encircles me, they pierce my hands and my feet ... They divide my clothes among them and cast lots for my garments'**
(vs 7,8,16,18).

What do you notice?

. . . . . . . . . . . . . . . . . . . . . . . . . . . . . . . . . . . . . . . . . . . . . . . . . .

. . . . . . . . . . . . . . . . . . . . . . . . . . . . . . . . . . . . . . . . . . . . . . . . . .

. . . . . . . . . . . . . . . . . . . . . . . . . . . . . . . . . . . . . . . . . . . . . . . . . .

. . . . . . . . . . . . . . . . . . . . . . . . . . . . . . . . . . . . . . . . . . . . . . . . . .

. . . . . . . . . . . . . . . . . . . . . . . . . . . . . . . . . . . . . . . . . . . . . . . . . .

. . . . . . . . . . . . . . . . . . . . . . . . . . . . . . . . . . . . . . . . . . . . . . . . . .

. . . . . . . . . . . . . . . . . . . . . . . . . . . . . . . . . . . . . . . . . . . . . . . . . .

. . . . . . . . . . . . . . . . . . . . . . . . . . . . . . . . . . . . . . . . . . . . . . . . . .

. . . . . . . . . . . . . . . . . . . . . . . . . . . . . . . . . . . . . . . . . . . . . . . . . .

. . . . . . . . . . . . . . . . . . . . . . . . . . . . . . . . . . . . . . . . . . . . . . . . . .

Jesus could have come down from that cross at any moment he chose.

What held him there?

How do you feel about this?

What questions do you have?

# Day 36

⁴⁵ From noon until three in the afternoon darkness came over all the land. ⁴⁶ About three in the afternoon Jesus cried out in a loud voice, 'Eli, Eli, lema sabachthani?' (which means 'My God, my God, why have you forsaken me?').[Ps 22:1]

⁴⁷ When some of those standing there heard this, they said, 'He's calling Elijah.'

⁴⁸ Immediately one of them ran and got a sponge. He filled it with wine vinegar, put it on a staff, and offered it to Jesus to drink. ⁴⁹ The rest said, 'Now leave him alone. Let's see if Elijah comes to save him.'

⁵⁰ And when Jesus had cried out again in a loud voice, he gave up his spirit.

⁵¹ At that moment the curtain of the temple was torn in two from top to bottom. The earth shook, the rocks split ⁵² and the tombs broke open. The bodies of many holy people who had died were raised to life. ⁵³ They came out of the tombs after Jesus' resurrection and went into the holy city and appeared to many people.

⁵⁴ When the centurion and those with him who were guarding Jesus saw the earthquake and all that had happened, they were terrified, and exclaimed, 'Surely he was the Son of God!'

⁵⁵ Many women were there, watching from a distance. They had followed Jesus from Galilee to care for his needs. ⁵⁶ Among them were Mary Magdalene, Mary the mother of James and Joseph, and the mother of Zebedee's sons.

Matthew 27:45–56

Jesus' death was so momentous that the whole earth shuddered (v 51).

What was going on?

Why was his last breath so significant?

. . . . . . . . . . . . . . . . . . . . . . . . . . . . . . . . . . . . . . . . . . . . . . . . . . . . .

. . . . . . . . . . . . . . . . . . . . . . . . . . . . . . . . . . . . . . . . . . . . . . . . . . . . .

. . . . . . . . . . . . . . . . . . . . . . . . . . . . . . . . . . . . . . . . . . . . . . . . . . . . .

. . . . . . . . . . . . . . . . . . . . . . . . . . . . . . . . . . . . . . . . . . . . . . . . . . . . .

. . . . . . . . . . . . . . . . . . . . . . . . . . . . . . . . . . . . . . . . . . . . . . . . . . . . .

. . . . . . . . . . . . . . . . . . . . . . . . . . . . . . . . . . . . . . . . . . . .

How has his death changed things for *you*?

# Day 36

The curtain in the Temple hung across the entrance to the inner sanctuary, and it ripped from top to bottom as Jesus died. From that moment on, God's people have free and direct access to his holy presence – including you.

Carve out some time to thank God for his incredible, unending love.

[57] As evening approached, there came a rich man from Arimathea, named Joseph, who had himself become a disciple of Jesus. [58] Going to Pilate, he asked for Jesus' body, and Pilate ordered that it be given to him. [59] Joseph took the body, wrapped it in a clean linen cloth, [60] and placed it in his own new tomb that he had cut out of the rock. He rolled a big stone in front of the entrance to the tomb and went away. [61] Mary Magdalene and the other Mary were sitting there opposite the tomb.

Matthew 27:57–61

# Day 37

The central principle of Christianity is that Jesus Christ died and was resurrected from the dead. From early on, people did their best to find other explanations for what happened – perhaps he did not quite die, or maybe grave robbers took the body, or the women returned to the wrong tomb. Matthew includes all sorts of details as evidence to support the claim that Jesus really did die.

Reflect on these details, and ask God to help you absorb the truth of what Jesus did for you.

. . . . . . . . . . . . . . . . . . . . . . . . . . . . . . . . . . . . . . . . .

. . . . . . . . . . . . . . . . . . . . . . . . . . . . . . . . . . . . . . . . .

. . . . . . . . . . . . . . . . . . . . . . . . . . . . . . . . . . . . . . . . .

. . . . . . . . . . . . . . . . . . . . . . . . . . . . . . . . . . . . . . . . .

. . . . . . . . . . . . . . . . . . . . . . . . . . . . . . . . . . . . . . . . .

. . . . . . . . . . . . . . . . . . . . . . . . . . . . . . . . . . . . . . . . .

. . . . . . . . . . . . . . . . . . . . . . . . . . . . . . . . . . . . . . . . .

. . . . . . . . . . . . . . . . . . . . . . . . . . . . . . . . . . . . . . . . .

. . . . . . . . . . . . . . . . . . . . . . . . . . . . . . . . . . . . . . . . .

. . . . . . . . . . . . . . . . . . . . . . . . . . . . . . . . . . . . . . . . .

. . . . . . . . . . . . . . . . . . . . . . . . . . . . . . . . . . . . . . . . .

. . . . . . . . . . . . . . . . . . . . . . . . . . . . . . . . . . . . . . . . .

. . . . . . . . . . . . . . . . . . . . . . . . . . . . . . . . . . . . . . . . .

. . . . . . . . . . . . . . . . . . . . . . . . . . . . . .

Take a moment to imagine how Mary (Jesus' mother) might have felt as she saw her son beaten, crucified and laid in a stranger's tomb.

........................................................................

........................................................................

........................................................................

........................................................................

........................................................................

........................................................................

........................................................................

........................................................................

Placing Jesus in the tomb seems like the end of the story. But God had a different plan. Never lose hope in what God has for you, even when it seems like it's the end of the story.

# Day 38

<sup>62</sup> The next day, the one after Preparation Day, the chief priests and the Pharisees went to Pilate. <sup>63</sup> 'Sir,' they said, 'we remember that while he was still alive that deceiver said, "After three days I will rise again." <sup>64</sup> So give the order for the tomb to be made secure until the third day. Otherwise, his disciples may come and steal the body and tell the people that he has been raised from the dead. This last deception will be worse than the first.'

<sup>65</sup> 'Take a guard,' Pilate answered. 'Go, make the tomb as secure as you know how.' <sup>66</sup> So they went and made the tomb secure by putting a seal on the stone and posting the guard.

Matthew 27:62–66

There are two groups of people particularly anxious to make sure that tomb is well guarded and that Jesus stays dead – the Romans and the religious leaders. Their desperation to prove that Jesus had been a fraud only served to make the evidence of his resurrection even stronger.

Do you believe that Jesus really died and that his body was secure in the tomb? Think carefully about the alternative theories. Are you happy with the evidence that refutes them?

# Day 38

Use the space to write a summary of your current beliefs around the events of the past few days.

. . . . . . . . . . . . . . . . . . . . . . . . . . . . . . . . . . . . . . . . . . . . . . . .

. . . . . . . . . . . . . . . . . . . . . . . . . . . . . . . . . . . . . . . . . . . . . . . .

. . . . . . . . . . . . . . . . . . . . . . . . . . . . . . . . . . . . . . . . . . . . . . . .

. . . . . . . . . . . . . . . . . . . . . . . . . . . . . . . . . . . . . . . . . . . . . . . .

. . . . . . . . . . . . . . . . . . . . . . . . . . . . . . . . . . . . . . . . . . . . . . . .

. . . . . . . . . . . . . . . . . . . . . . . . . . . . . . . . . . . . . . . . . . . . . . . .

. . . . . . . . . . . . . . . . . . . . . . . . . . . . . . . . . . . . . . . . . . . . . . . .

. . . . . . . . . . . . . . . . . . . . . . . . . . . . . . . . . . . . . . . . . . . . . . . .

. . . . . . . . . . . . . . . . . . . . . . . . . . . . . . . . . . . . . . . . . . . . . . . .

. . . . . . . . . . . . . . . . . . . . . . . . . . . . . . . . . . . . . . . . . . . . . . . .

. . . . . . . . . . . . . . . . . . . . . . . . . . . . . . . . . . . . . . . . . . . . . . . .

. . . . . . . . . . . . . . . . . . . . . . . . . . . . . . . . . . . . . . . . . . . . . . . .

. . . . . . . . . . . . . . . . . . . . . . . . . . . . . . . . . . . . . . . . . . . . . . . .

. . . . . . . . . . . . . . . . . . . . . . . . . . . . . . . . . . . . . . . . . . . . . . . .

. . . . . . . . . . . . . . . . . . . . . . . . . . . . .

After the Sabbath, at dawn on the first day of the week, Mary Magdalene and the other Mary went to look at the tomb.

[2] There was a violent earthquake, for an angel of the Lord came down from heaven and, going to the tomb, rolled back the stone and sat on it. [3] His appearance was like lightning, and his clothes were white as snow. [4] The guards were so afraid of him that they shook and became like dead men.

[5] The angel said to the women, 'Do not be afraid, for I know that you are looking for Jesus, who was crucified. [6] He is not here; he has risen, just as he said. Come and see the place where he lay. [7] Then go quickly and tell his disciples: "He has risen from the dead and is going ahead of you into Galilee. There you will see him." Now I have told you.'

[8] So the women hurried away from the tomb, afraid yet filled with joy, and ran to tell his disciples. [9] Suddenly Jesus met them. 'Greetings,' he said. They came to him, clasped his feet and worshipped him. [10] Then Jesus said to them, 'Do not be afraid. Go and tell my brothers to go to Galilee; there they will see me.'

Matthew 28:1–10

# Day 39

Although Jesus had predicted his resurrection on the third day, rationality had taken over and no one expected to see him again in the flesh. Mark and Luke tell us the women were bringing spices, hoping to complete the appropriate burial ritual.

The revealing of the empty tomb is suitably dramatic: an earthquake, a blindingly bright angel, the rolling away of the stone, the guards in shock and terror. Imagine how you might have felt if you had been there.

And then... Jesus himself – a risen Jesus, full of life – a Jesus still alive who we can know NOW, through the Holy Spirit, and who one day we will see face to face.

Take a moment to reflect on the promise of heaven. Imagine what it will be like to see Jesus face to face.

# Day 40

<sup>16</sup> Then the eleven disciples went to Galilee, to the mountain where Jesus had told them to go. <sup>17</sup> When they saw him, they worshipped him; but some doubted. <sup>18</sup> Then Jesus came to them and said, 'All authority in heaven and on earth has been given to me. <sup>19</sup> Therefore go and make disciples of all nations, baptising them in the name of the Father and of the Son and of the Holy Spirit, <sup>20</sup> and teaching them to obey everything I have commanded you. And surely I am with you always, to the very end of the age.'

Matthew 28:16–20

Jesus promises to equip us to continue in his mission.

How do you feel about being a disciple maker?

Spend some time asking Jesus to help you trust in him.

. . . . . . . . . . . . . . . . . . . . . . . . . . . . . . . . . . . . . . . . . .

. . . . . . . . . . . . . . . . . . . . . . . . . . . . . . . . . . . . . . . . . .

. . . . . . . . . . . . . . . . . . . . . . . . . . . . . . . . . . . . . . . . . .

. . . . . . . . . . . . . . . . . . . . . . . . . . . . . . . . . . . . . . . . . .

. . . . . . . . . . . . . . . . . . . . . . . . . . . . . . . . . . . . . . . . . .

. . . . . . . . . . . . . . . . . . . . . . . . . . . . . . . . . . . . . . . . . .

. . . . . . . . . . . . . . . . . . . . . . . . . . . . . . . . . . . . . . . . . .

. . . . . . . . . . . . . . . . . . . . . . . . . . . . . . . . . . . . . . . . . .

. . . . . . . . . . . . . . . . . . . . . . . . . . . . . . . . . . . . . . . . . .

. . . . . . . . . . . . . . . . . . . . . . . . . . . . . . . . . . . . . . . . . .

. . . . . . . . . . . . . . . . . . . . . . . . . . . . . . . . . . . . . . . . . .

. . . . . . . . . . . . . . . . . . . . . . . . . . . . . . . . . . . . . . . . . .

. . . . . . . . . . . . . . . . . . . . . . . . . . . . . . . . . . . . . . . . . .

. . . . . . . . . . . . . . . . . . . . . . . . . . . . . . .

# Day 40

Think back over the last 39 days.

What have you learned about God that you didn't know before?

What has God spoken to you about?

How will the next 40 days be different, given what you've learned?

. . . . . . . . . . . . . . . . . . . . . . . . . . . . . . . . . . . . . . . . . . . . . . . . . . . . . . . . . . . . . . . . . .

. . . . . . . . . . . . . . . . . . . . . . . . . . . . . . . . . . . . . . . . . . . . . . . . . . . . . . . . . . . . . . . . . .

. . . . . . . . . . . . . . . . . . . . . . . . . . . . . . . . . . . . . . . . . . . . . . . . . . . . . . . . . . . . . . . . . .

. . . . . . . . . . . . . . . . . . . . . . . . . . . . . . . . . . . . . . . . . . . . . . . . . . . . . . . . . . . . . . . . . .

. . . . . . . . . . . . . . . . . . . . . . . . . . . . . . . . . . . . . . . . . . . . . . . . . . . . . . . . . . . . . . . . . .

. . . . . . . . . . . . . . . . . . . . . . . . . . . . . . . . . . . . . . . . . . . . . . . . . . . . . . . . . . . . . . . . . .

. . . . . . . . . . . . . . . . . . . . . . . . . . . . . . . . . . . . . . . . . . . . . . . . . . . . . . . . . . . . . . . . . .

. . . . . . . . . . . . . . . . . . . . . . . . . . . . . . . . . . . . . . . . . . . . . . . . . . . . . . . . . . . . . . . . . .

. . . . . . . . . . . . . . . . . . . . . . . . . . . . . . . . . . . . . . . . . . . . . . . . . . . . . . . . . .

**What will your next step be in your journey of faith?**

# Notes

# Notes

........................................
........................................
........................................
........................................
........................................
........................................
........................................
........................................
........................................
........................................
........................................
........................................
........................................
........................................
........................................
........................................
........................................
........................................
........................................
..................

# Notes